SPANISH
InteriorDesign

The Deutsche Nationalbibliothek lists this publication in the Deutsche Nationalbibliografie; detailed bibliographical data are available on the internet at http://dnb.d-nb.de.

ISBN 978-3-03768-069-8
© 2011 by Braun Publishing AG
www.braun-publishing.ch

1st edition 2011

Michelle Galindo (English and Spanish editing texts)
Graphic concept: Michaela Prinz, Berlin

SPANISH

InteriorDesign

Michelle Galindo

BRAUN

Content | Contenido

Splashes of Flamenco, golden beaches, sunshine, siestas and fiestas...Fortunately, the clichés about Spain are reinterpreted inside the interiors presented in this book; through the innovative trends which are associated with values, like sustainability and the individual concept of it; the intimate human comfort and playful concepts all stand out for "the simplicity and creativity of the ideas put forward" as well as for its functionality. It is a reflection of the quality of living. Spanish Interior Design offers a glimpse into a wide range of interiors from private homes to museums, from classical to contemporary, representing the contrasts and emotions and its varied architectural styles which are a result of many influences through the centuries, from Gothic, Islamic to Moorish interiors, and silverwork and ornate interiors. The projects featured in this volume explore a balance of an aesthetic link between the past and the future, thus respecting the original turn-of-the-century tile work and ornate moldings found in some projects and adding the new elements, such as pieces that have been meticulously chosen or designed to give every venue its own character. It features the work of leading and established Spanish interior designers, such as Jaime Hayon, who not only blurs the lines between art and design, but also questions what design actually is

Un toque de Flamenco, playas de oro, luz del sol, siestas y fiestas... Por suerte, los clichés sobre España son reinterpretados dentro de los interiores presentados en este libro; a través de las tendencias innovadoras que son asociadas con valores, como la sostenibilidad y su concepto individual; la íntima comodidad humana y conceptos divertidos se destacan por "la simplicidad y la creatividad de las ideas propuestas" así como por su funcionalidad. Esto es una reflexión de la calidad de vida. El diseño interior español ofrece una vislumbre en una amplia gama de interiores desde casas privadas a museos, de clásico a contemporáneo, representando los contrastes y emociones y sus estilos arquitectónicos variados que son el resultado de muchas influencias durante los siglos, desde interiores Góticos, Islámicos a árabes. Los proyectos destacados en este volumen exploran el equilibrio de un eslabón estético entre el pasado y el futuro, así mismo respetan el trabajo de azulejo original "la vuelta del siglo" y moldeados adornados encontrados en algunos proyectos y añaden elementos nuevos, como piezas que han sido meticulosamente escogidas o diseñadas para darle a cada lugar su propio carácter. Spanish Interior Design presenta el trabajo de diseñadores de interiores destacados y establecidos, como Jaime Hayon, que no sólo enturbia las

by pushing the boundaries of the materials and Patricia Urquiola, who combines sumptuous textiles with elegant materials and a rich palette of colors to create sophisticated and vibrant living spaces. Dear Design opts instead for taut yet dazzling simplicity, breaking down barriers between art and technicality. The interiors embody a new type of creative Renaissance designers who, thanks to their interdisciplinary approach and extraordinary talent, can realize their unique stylistic language across various areas and media. This book aims to create a global vision of interior design in Spain today, featuring 47 of the best creative, forefront designs which are a result of a stylish blend of simplicity and sophistication effortlessly mixing Mediterranean influences. Spain is edging ever closer to reigning in the design cutting edge crown.

líneas entre el arte y el diseño, pero también cuestiona lo que en realidad es el diseño, empujando las fronteras de los materiales y Patricia Urquiola, quien combina el textil suntuoso con materiales elegantes y una paleta rica de colores para crear espacios vitales sofisticados y vibrantes. Dear Design opta en cambio por la simplicidad tensa, pero deslumbrante y rompe las barreras entre el arte y lo técnico. Los interiores incorporan un nuevo tipo de diseñadores creativos de Renacimiento quien, gracias a su enfoque interdisciplinario y talento extraordinario, pueden realizar su propio idioma estilístico a través de varias áreas y medios de comunicación. Este libro propone crear una visión global del diseño de hoy de interiores en España, presentando 47 de los mejores diseños de vanguardia creativos que son el resultado de una mezcla elegante de simplicidad y sofisticación que sin esfuerzo alguno mezcla influencias mediterráneas. España esta cada vez más cerca al borde del reinado de la corona de vanguardia de diseño.

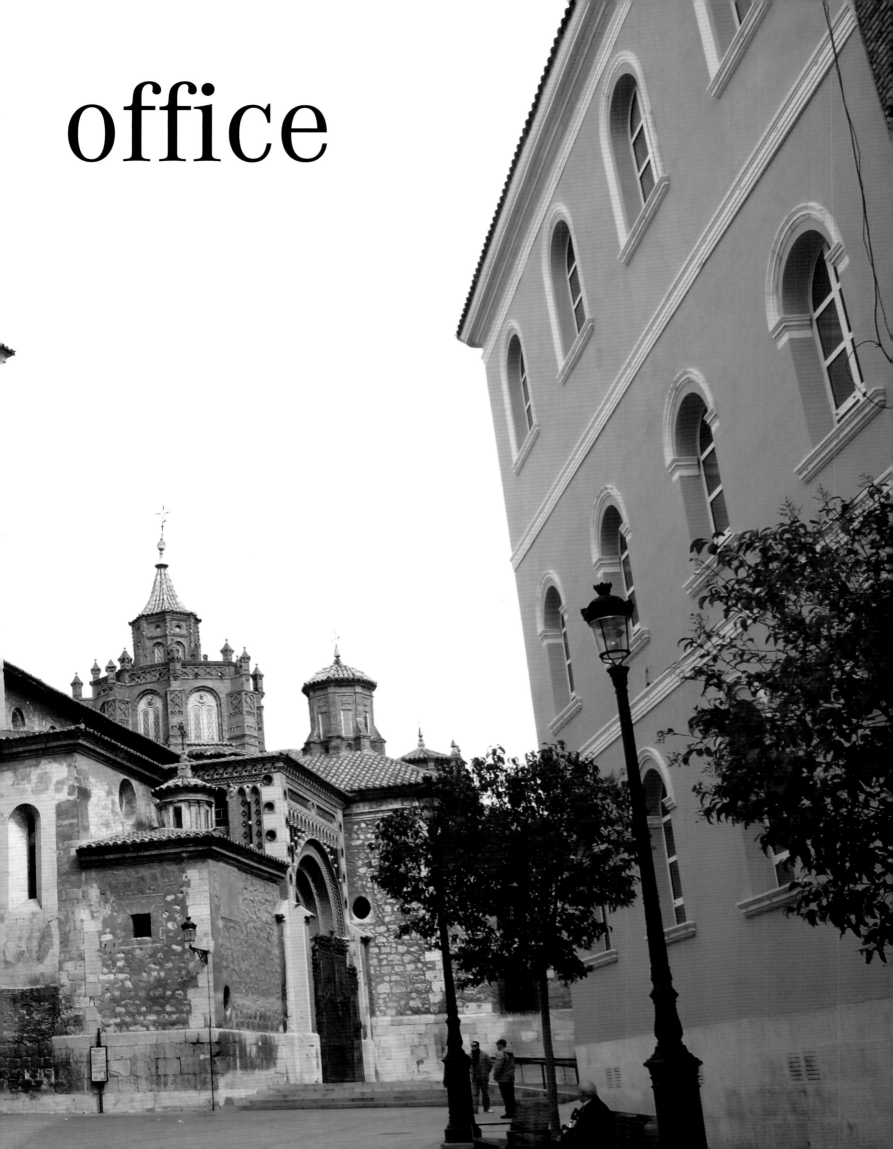

office

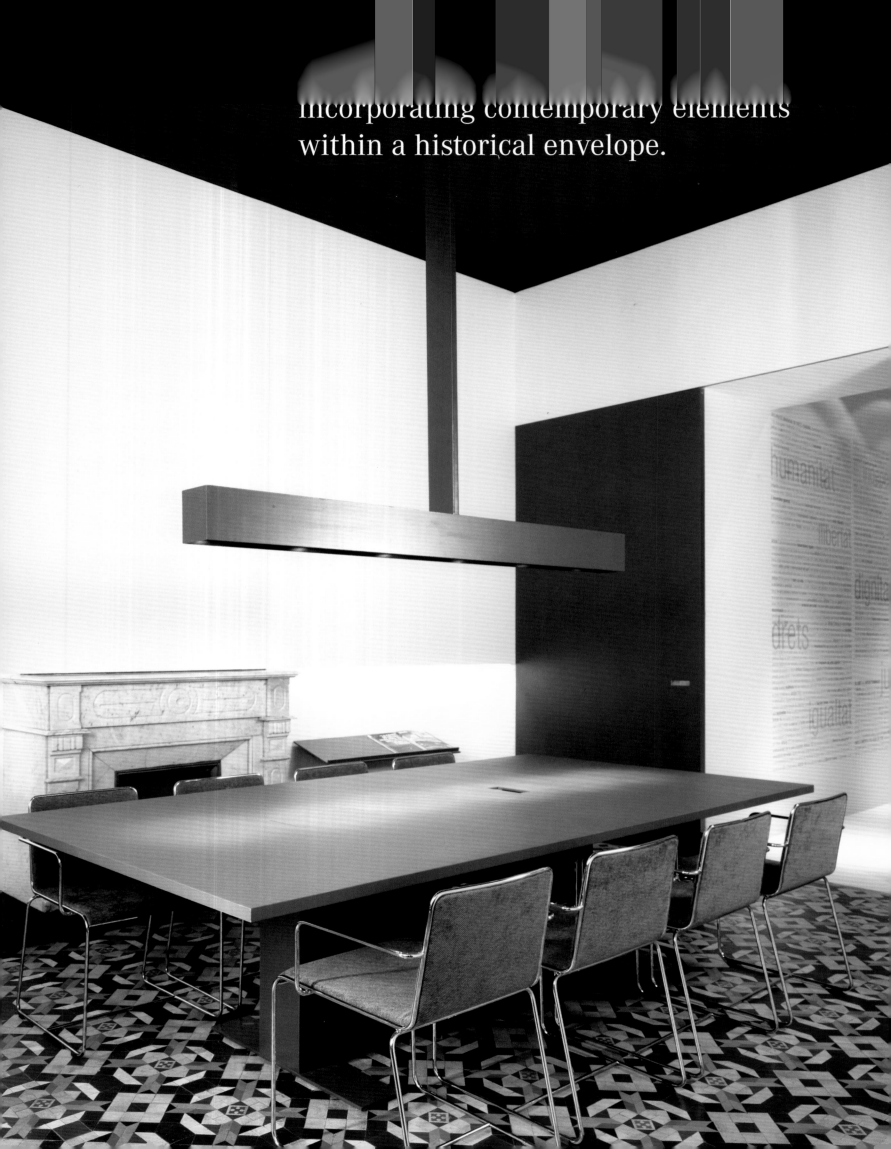

incorporating contemporary elements
within a historical envelope.

InDret

Francesc Rifé

Location: Barcelona. **Client:** COAATM. **Completion:** 2007. **Main function:** Office. **Materials:** Smoked glass mirrors.

A floor of an early 20th century building in the historical center of Vilafranca del Penedès, was renovated to house the new central office of InDret. The building's main façade has a noble look, while the other side opens to an unattractive backyard located 1.60 meters below ground level. This court was renovated as well. A great longitudinal 60 centimeter wall forms a structural axle, determining the location of the bathrooms for men and women. Featuring smoked glass mirrors; these bathrooms resemble cockpits, and are designed as two "suspended" boxes located below the rest of the building.

Un piso en un edificio de principios del siglo 20, ubicado en el centro histórico de Vilafranca del Penedès, fue renovado para alojar la nueva oficina central de InDret, un despacho de abogados. La fachada principal del edificio es noble, mientras el otro lado se abre hacia un patio trasero un poco atractivo ubicado a 1.60 metros de nivel subterráneo. En su intervencion se introdujo una pared de 60 centímetros como eje estructural, determinando la posición de los baños: los cuales fueron diseñados como dos cajas "suspendidas", parecidas a cabinas de pilotos y localizadas debajo del resto del edificio.

← Conference room. Sala de conferencia.

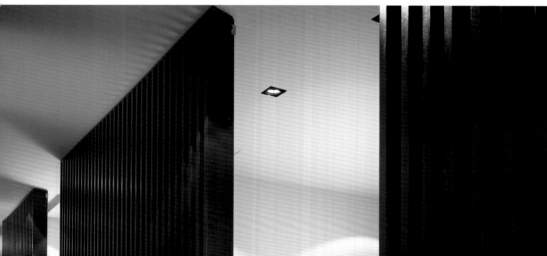

↖ View into offices. Vista hacia las oficinas.
↑ View into office through slit wall. Vista hacia la oficina a traves de rejilla.
← Office. Oficina.
↓ Typical floor plan. Planta típica.
→ Reception area. Vestíbulo.

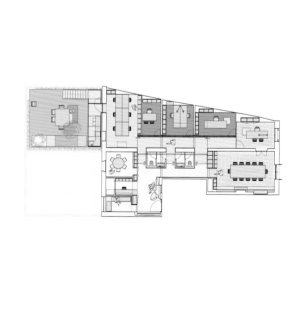

Typical of Spanish interior design is...
to find a sequence to maintain the
privacy of the spaces.

Edificio Judicial

Estudio MMASA | Patricia Muñiz + Luciano Alfaya

Address: El Barco de Valdeorras, Orense. **Client:** Xunta de Galicia. **Completion:** 2010. **Main function:** Court building. **Materials:** Linoleum, granite, wood and glass.

The main face of the court building is a constant fold of sheets of aluminium with a chromatic progression that is interrupted by vertical hollows protected by broken muds. These are diminishing progressively in height causing the incident of the light to be greater and on the contrary, the thermal control of the building turns out to be more important. In the interior the visitors area is covered in wood, the artificial lighting is combined with a great central skylight that separates visually the public zone and defendants of the judges' area. The vertical parameters are the main elelement, painted in white to serve as major reflection of the light; these create spaces of different dimensions depending on the estimated use of the areas. These sequences serve as indirect comprehension of the degree of privacy of every stay and are reflected in the exterior image, helping to distinguish the building in the urban set on which it is located.

La fachada principal del edificio de juzgados es un pliegue continuo de láminas de aluminio con una progresión cromática que se interrumpe por huecos verticales protegidos por lamas quebradas. Estos van progresivamente disminuyendo en su altura ya que la incidencia de la luz será mayor y, por el contrario, resulta más importante el control térmico del edificio. Interiormente, en las Salas de Visitas acabadas en madera, se combina la iluminación artificial con un gran lucernario central que separa visualmente la zona de público y acusados del área de jueces. Los paramentros verticales son el elemento principal, generalmente en lacados y pintados de blanco para la mayor reflexión de la luz, crean espacios de diferentes dimensiones en función del uso estimado de las áreas. Estas secuencias sirven como comprensión indirecta del grado de privacidad de cada estancia y se ven reflejadas en la imagen exterior, contribuyendo a singularizar el edificio en el conjunto urbano en el que se asienta.

← Reception area. Vestíbulo.

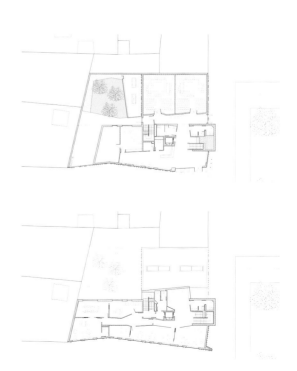

↖ Hallway leading to visitor's area. Pasillo hacia sala de visitas.

↑ Court room. Sala de tribunal.

← Restricted area. Zona restringida.

↓ Ground floor plan and typical floor plan. Planta baja y planta típica.

→ Office room. Oficina.

Typical of Spanish interior design is...
to preserve its history and unify it
with a new design.

COAATM

Díaz y Díaz Arquitectos

Address: Calle del Maestro Victoria 3, 28013 Madrid. **Client:** COAATM. **Completion:** 2008, original: 1906. **Main function:** Office. **Materials:** Bamboo coatings, ceramic pavements and stucco ceilings.

The generating idea of the architectural project has been given by the characteristics of the building to rehabilitate and to consider its floor plan which was generated from a central core formed by both courtyards and the main stairs; consistently, with the aim to provide with coherence to its set, it was decided to border and uniformal contribution of details, finishes and textures in a solid and quality frame, according to the category of the building. The central core of the courts and main stairs constitutes the element from which it is organized and developed the floor plan of the building, by what was decided to rehabilitate its interior by a wooden bamboo surface to create a big contrast with the rest of the walls, painted white color with the aim to promote the entry of the natural light in the interior spaces, emphasizing his height and promoting his conditions of habitability.

La idea generadora del proyecto arquitectónico ha sido, dadas las características del edificio a rehabilitar, evidenciar su planta canónica generada alrededor de un núcleo central formado por los dos patios y la escalera principal y, consecuentemente, con el objetivo de dotar de coherencia a su conjunto, se decidió limitar y uniformar la aportación de detalles, acabados y texturas, en un marco de solidez y calidad, acorde con la categoría del edificio. El núcleo central de patios y escalera principales constituye el elemento alrededor del cual se organiza y desarrolla la planta del edificio, por lo que se decidió revestirlo en su interior con un empanelado de madera de "bamboo" que, debido a su exotismo y color, contrasta fuertemente con el resto de las paredes, pintadas de color blanco con el objetivo de potenciar la entrada de la luz natural en los espacios interiores, enfatizando su altura y potenciando sus condiciones de habitabilidad.

← Mezzanine, reception area. Entreplanta, recepción.

↖ Library terrace. Terraza de la biblioteca.
↑ Lateral stairs. Escaleras laterales.
← Lateral stairs – second floor. Escaleras laterales – segunda planta.
↗ Reception. Recepción.
↘ Fourth floor plan. Cuarta planta.
↘↘ Mezzanine. Entreplanta.

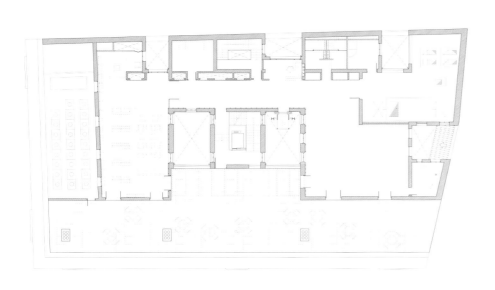

hotel, bar, restau

rant

Typical of Spanish interior design is...
to emphasize the connection between the different elements of the interior.

Hotel Alexandra

Estudi Borrell

Address: Calle Mallorca 251, 08008 Barcelona. **Client:** Diagonal Hotels. **Completion:** 2008. **Main function:** Hotel, restaurant, bar. **Materials:** Recycled polished glass floors, reflecting crystal white ceilings and wooden walls.

The Hotel Alexandra brings together architecture, design of forefront and comfort at the level of the most demanding clients. The challenge has been to create a unique space which would adapt to the different needs of the clients throughout the day. Different environments that interact thanks to the diversity of pieces of furniture – as the multiple combinations of the sofa Tufty-Time, designed by Patricia Urquiola for B&B Italia and of lighting. As the great chandelier – designed by Bocci especially for this project, emphasizing the connection between the different elements of its interior and that is one of the pieces that give great personality to the hotel.

El Hotel Alexandra conjuga arquitectura, diseño de vanguardia y confort a la altura de los clientes más exigentes. El reto ha sido crear un único espacio que se adecuara a las distintas necesidades de los clientes a lo largo del día. Distintos ambientes que interaccionan gracias a la diversidad de piezas de mobiliario -como las múltiples combinaciones del sofá Tufty-Time, diseño de Patricia Urquiola para B&B Italia- y de iluminación. Como el gran candelabro -diseñado por Bocci especialmente para este proyecto- que enfatiza la conexión entre los distintos elementos de su interior y que es una de las piezas que dan gran personalidad al hotel.

← Lobby with view to street. Vestíbulo con vista a la calle.

↖ DaLuca Bar. Bar DaLuca.
↑ DaLuca Restaurant. Restaurante DaLuca.
← Double-height ceilings in breakfast room. Techos de doble altura en el comedor del desayuno.
↗ Detail of breakfast table. Detalle del comedor del desayuno.
↘ Lobby featuring a Tufty-Time sofa by Patricia Urquiola for B&B Italia. Vestíbulo que destaca un sofá de Tufty-Time diseño de Patricia Urquiola para B&B Italia.
↘↘ Entrance way. Entrada.

Typical of Spanish interior design is...
the combination of art and passion.

Restaurant Xup Xup

Molins Interiors

Address: Calle Córcega 261, 08036 Barcelona. **Client:** Grupo Arts Catering. **Completion:** 2009. **Graphic Design:** Alex Verdaguer. **Main function:** Restaurant. **Furniture, tapestries for the benches, curtains and cushions:** Molins Interiors.

The restaurant is distributed across three rooms that honor those utensils which have lasted decade after decade, such as the wine bottle, the mortar or the wine boot, among others. In the first room, the objects which are related to the wine and to the champagne are the main protagonists. In this respect one of the walls has been covered with cork used in the big barrels. Wine bottles turned into table lamps. Linens made out of the fabric of "mocador of fer farcells" explode in walls and ceiling, being the basic colors of the handkerchief (the black, orange and dark brown) the chromatic influence of the space. In the second room, it is the mortar and its green and yellow colors which are founded on the space, across the walls, chairs and cushions. Finally, in a private room, next to the second room, the wine boot and its colors of reference are to be honoured, featuring black and natural skin and reinterpreting the great classic boot as a main lamp.

El restaurante se distribuye a través de tres salas que le dan homenaje a aquellos utensilios cuya utilidad ha perdurado década tras década tales como el porrón, el mortero o la bota de vino, entre otros. En la primera sala, los objetos entorno al vino y al cava son los grandes protagonistas. En este sentido se ha recubierto una de las paredes a base de tapones de corcho antiguos empleados en las grandes barricas. Porrones de vino convertidos en lámparas de mesa. Lienzos realizados con la tela del "mocador de fer farcells" explosionan en paredes y techo, siendo los colores básicos del pañuelo (el negro, el naranja y el marrón) la influencia cromática del espacio. En la segunda sala, es el mortero y sus colores verdes y amarillos quienes se funden en el espacio, a través de las paredes, sillas y cojines. Por último, en el privé contiguo a la segunda sala, se ha querido homenajear a la bota de vino, y a sus colores de referencia más castizos como el rojo, el negro y la piel natural, reinterpretando un gran clásico de la bota a modo de lamparón principal.

← View to high tables with lamps made out of three wine bottles. Mesas altas con lámparas a base de tres porrones de vino.

↑ Wall display. Mostrador de porrones de vino.
← Detail lamp. Detalle de lampara.
→ Interior view. Vista del interior.
↘ View towards the bar. Vista hacia la barra.
↘↘ Wall surface covered with cork. Pared recubierta a base de tapones de corcho.

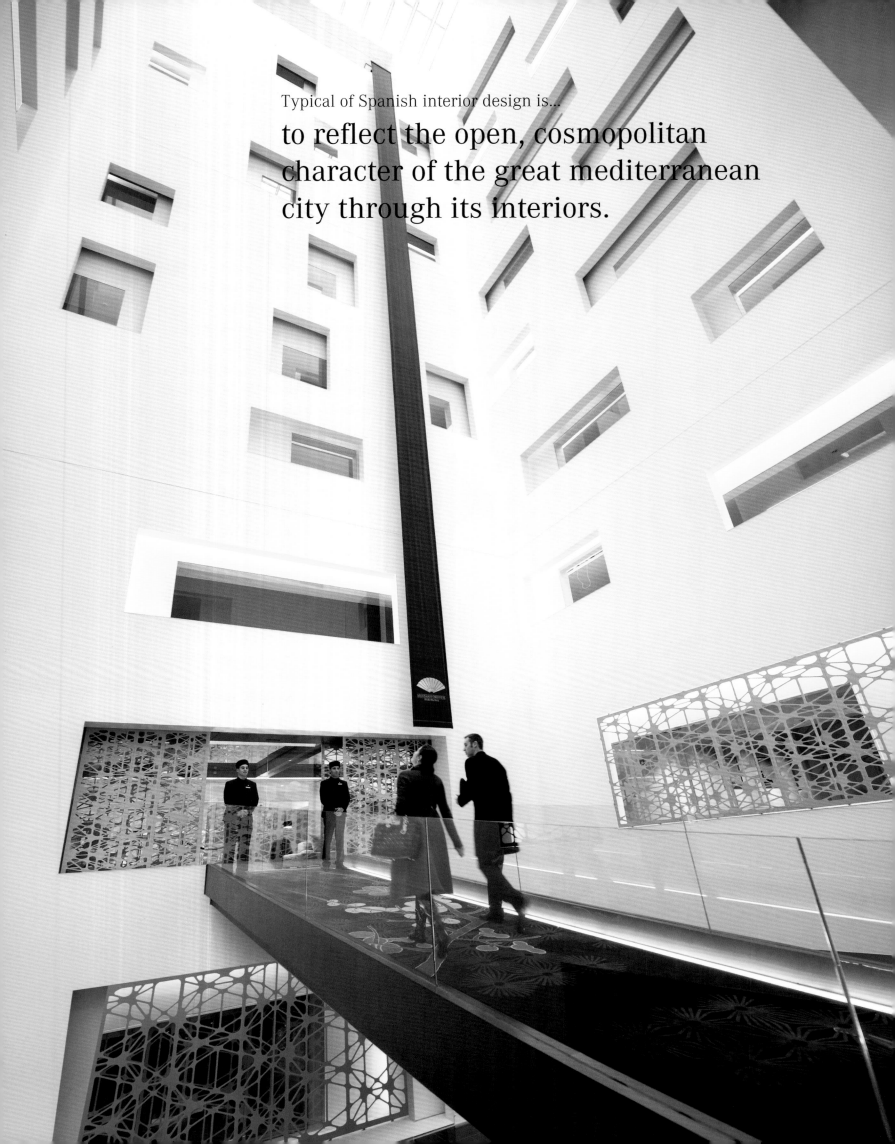

Typical of Spanish interior design is...
to reflect the open, cosmopolitan
character of the great mediterranean
city through its interiors.

Mandarin Oriental Hotel

Patricia Urquiola / OAB (Office of Architecture in Barcelona)

Address: Passeig de Gràcia 38–40, 08007 Barcelona. **Client:** Mandarin Oriental Hotels. **Completion:** 2009. **Main function:** Hotel, restaurant and spa. **Materials:** Light oak floors, mosaics by Mutina and Bisazza and colored glass.

This new luxury hotel is situated in an elegant mid 20th-century former bank building, recreated with a highly stylised contemporary interior. The spatial layout and furniture design, ceiling decoration and the beautiful hand-woven carpets, reminiscent of the charm and distinction of great classical hotels, have all been carefully chosen by Patricia Urquiola. Nearly all the furniture has been specifically designed by the designer or adapted for the hotel in conjunction with such famous names as B&B Italia, DePadova, Flos and Moroso. From the Scandinavian style armchairs in Moments restaurant, the lobby sofa, which has been adapted from a traditional Chesterfield, the tartan carpet reminiscent of the Gentleman's Clubs of bygone days which adorns the Banker's Bar floor, to the fully restored early 20th century French ironing table which serves as a centerpiece to Blanc restaurant and lounge; each piece has been meticulously chosen or designed to give every venue its own character.

Este nuevo hotel de lujo esta situado en un antiguo, elegante edificio bancario de mediados del siglo XX, recreado con un interior sumamente estilizado contemporáneo. La disposición espacial y el diseño de muebles, las decoraciones de techo y las alfombras hermosas tejidas a mano, evocadoras del encanto y la distinción de grandes hoteles clásicos, han sido eligidos todos por la diseñadora Urquiola. Casi todos los muebles han sido diseñados específicamente por la diseñadora o adaptados para el hotel en la conjunción con tales nombres famosos como B&B Italia, DePadova, Flos y Moroso. Desde las butacas de estilo escandinavas en Moments restaurant, el sofá del vestíbulo, que ha sido adaptado de un Chesterfield tradicional, la alfombra de tartán evocadora que adornan el suelo del Banker's Bar, hasta la mesa francesa de planchar de principios del siglo XX, totalmente restaurada que sirve como una pieza central en el restaurante Blanc y lounge; cada pieza ha sido meticulosamente escogida o diseñada para dar le un carácter propio a cada lugar.

← Atrium ramp at entrance leading to the restaurant and lounge.
Atrio con rampa a la entrada que dirige hacia el restaurante y el salón.

↖ Mandarin Terrace guest room. Habitación Mandarin Terrace.
↑ Pool area with a large malachite-green screen. Piscina con una pantalla verde de malaquita grande.
← En-suite bathroom. Baño en-suite.
↗ Interior with rectangular, metallic grid, allowing for greater privacy. Interior con rejilla rectangular, metálica para permitir mas privacidad.
↘ Dining area with view to kitchen. Comedor con vista hacia la cocina.
↘↘ Waiting area in spa. Sala de espera en el spa.

Typical of Spanish interior design is...

to find equilibrium in history, art,
wellbeing and rest.

Hospes Palacio de Bailio

Hospes Design

Address: Ramírez de las Casas Deza 10–12, 14001 Córdoba. **Client:** Hospes. **Completion:** 2006. **Main function:** Hotel, spa, restaurant/bar.
Materials: Wrought-iron balcony railings and terracotta tiles.

Built between the 16th and 18th century this traditional Andalusian agrarian estate has been meticulously restored and finely balanced with contemporary design. Original detailing such as wrought-iron balcony railings, terracotta tiles, Moorish decorative elements and a lavishly painted ceiling have been artfully combined with understated modern touches at the Hospes Palacio del Bailio in Cordoba. Rich fabrics and textures in champagne and copper tones are offset by dark walnut wood and light polished marble floors throughout the interiors – solid slabs of black stone from Cordoba lead to the gardens outside, thus creating a stylistic bridge from the interior to the exterior. The restoration of paintings and frescos from the 19th century is a further example of the care and attention given to the revitalisation of past beauty at the Hospes Palacio del Bailío.

Construido entre el siglo XVI y XVIII este agrario tradicional Andaluz ha sido restaurado meticulosamente y equilibrado con el diseño contemporáneo. Detallados originales como rieles del balcón de hierro forjado, azulejos de terracota, elementos decorativos Moros y un esplendido techo pintado fueron ingeniosamente combinados con toques minimizados modernos en el Hospes Palacio del Bailio en Córdoba. Telas de lujo y texturas en color champán y tonos de cobre se compensan por la madera de nuez oscura y alumbran los pisos pulidos de mármol a traves de los interiores - las losas sólidas de piedra negra de Córdoba te transportan a los jardines de afuera, así mismo creando un puente estilístico del interior al exterior. La restauración de las pinturas y frescos del siglo 19 es un remoto ejemplo del cuidado y de la atención dada a la revitalización del pasado.

← Deluxe guest room. Habitación Deluxe.

↖ Suite featuring original paintings of the 18th century such as scenes of the El Quijote. Suite con pinturas originales del siglo XVIII con escenas de El Quijote.

↑ Living room. Sala de estar.

← Hallway. Pasillo.

→ Lobby. Vestíbulo.

Typical of Spanish interior design is...

an authentic and pure mixture
of new and old elements.

Hospes Hotel Palacio de los Patos

Hospes Design

Address: Calle de Solarillo de Gracia 1, 18002 Granada. **Client:** Hospes. **Completion:** 2005. **Main function:** Hotel, spa, restaurant/bar. **Materials:** Stone, glass and metal.

The Hospes Palacio de los Patos yokes a 19th century classic palace to an uncompromising modern new wing of design scheme. The language of the interior design chosen for the rooms reflects the desire to highlight the original proportions of the building, integrating them with a new, distinctive identity of multicultural progressive design. White or black coconut leather is used throughout the interiors, combined with silver and stainless steel details. Light materials and shades are added to weightless textures of wood and stone, fitting in perfectly with the symmetrical compositions of the rooms. In the five suites, a veritable overflow of silver has been introduced as a key-unifying element in the design. Silver curtains, carpets, chairs and details contrast brilliantly with the bright purple chaise-longues that breathe life into the almost monochrome surroundings.

El Hospes Palacio de los Patos une a un palacio del siglo XIX al diseño de un nuevo esquema de la ala nueva. La lengua del diseño interior escogido para los espacios refleja el deseo de destacar las dimensiones originales del edificio, la integración ellos con una identidad nueva, distintiva de diseño multicultural progresivo. El cuero blanco o negro de coco es usado en todas partes de los interiores, combinados con detalles de acero inoxidable y la plata. Materiales ligeros y sombras son añadidos a las texturas ingrávidas de madera y piedra, que cabe perfectamente con las composiciones simétricas de los espacios. En las cinco suites, un desbordamiento verdadero de plata ha sido presentado como una llave que unifica el elemento en el diseño. Cortinas de plata, alfombras, presiden y el contraste de detalles intensamente con el brillante púrpura contraste intensamente con las chaise longue brillantes púrpuras que respiran la vida en el entorno casi monocromo.

← Foyer with skylight. Vestíbulo con claraboya.

↖ Senzone Restaurant. Restaurante Senzone.
↑ Grand Suite. Grand Suite.
← Living room. Salón.
↗ Presidential Suite. Suite Pesidencial.
↘ Alabaster-white interior. Interior blanco de alabastro.
↘↘ Pool area. Piscina.

Typical of Spanish interior design is...

blending art and design in
an elegant and delicate way.

La Terraza del Casino

Hayon Studio/Jaime Hayon

Address: Calle Alcala 15, 28014 Madrid. **Client:** NH Hotels. **Completion:** 2007. **Main function:** Restaurant. **Materials:** Marble, mirrors, lacquered wood, colored glass and ceramics.

The Restaurant La Terraza del Casino explores the balance of an aesthetic link between past and future using a very personal style that connects harmoniously with the imaginative and innovative kitchen of the outstanding chef: Paco Roncero. The project presents new furniture elements created by Hayon in consonance with the restaurant's needs as well as different hand crafted details. To recreate the space: huge handmade ceramic chandeliers, recycled black and white floors from Bisazza, different styles of chairs which are only unified on their finishing level, long and elegant theatrical curtains; a wall covered with diamond mirrors to create reflections and gray colors accentuated by details of color.

El Restaurante La Terraza del el Casino explora el equilibrio de un eslabón estético entre el pasado y futuro que usa un estilo muy personal que se une armoniosamente con la cocina imaginativa e innovadora del excepcional: Paco Roncero. El proyecto presenta nuevos elementos de muebles creados por Hayon que cumplen con las necesidades del restaurante así como ciertos detalles hechos a mano. En la intervencion del espacio se agregaron enormes candelabros de luces hechas a mano de cerámica, pisos reciclados blancos y negros de Bisazza, diferentes estilos de sillas, cortinas teatrales largas y; una pared cubierta con espejos en forma de diamante para crear reflexiones y con colores grises acentuados por los detalles del color.

← Interior featuring handmade ceramic chandeliers and recycled black and white Bisazza crystal floors. Interior con chandeliers de ceramica realizados a mano y suelos de Bisazza con placas blancas y negras creadas con cristal reciclado.

↖ Wall covered in diamond-shape mirrors. Pared recubierta con espejos de forma de diamante.
↑ Interior detail. Detalle del interior.
← Main entrance. Entrada principal.
↗ Interior view. Vista hacia el interior.
↘ Floor plan. Planta.
↘↘ Lobby. Vestíbulo.

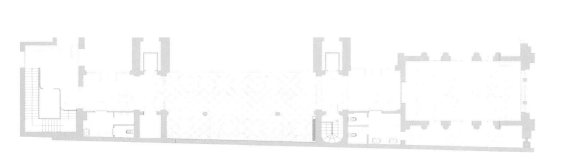

Typical of Spanish interior design is...
to add a dynamic element, such as the
legendary barrette or Spanish comb.

Estado Puro

James & Mau Arquitectura

Address: Plaza Cánovas del Castillo 4, 28014 Madrid. **Completion:** 2009. **Advertising design of Mahou beer brand:** James & Mau Arquitectura, in collaboration with the Agency Full Mix. **Artistic installation:** NI and James & Mau atelier (door frame). **Main function:** Restaurant. **Materials:** 1000 barrettes as a ceiling and wall and marble bar. **Art:** Images of Mahou beer advertising of the 1940s.

The architectural firm James & Mau designed a "typical" Spanish restaurant in the center of Madrid. Located on the paseo del Prado in the heart of Madrid, Estado Puro was designed for Paco Roncero - one of Spain's cutting edge chef, who respects the foundations of the Spanish cuisine while experimenting with food. The chef's sensitivity towards new cuisine would form the starting point for James & Mau. It resulted in a concept that unites tradition with innovation without becoming kitsch. The key element would be the barrette, a Spanish folklore object that is all but forgotten in Madrid souvenir stores. 1,000 Barrettes were used to create a retro illuminated skin that forms a wall and ceiling covering.

La firma arquitectónica de James & Mau diseñó un restaurante 'típico' español en el centro de Madrid. Localizado sobre el paseo del Prado en el corazón de Madrid, Estado Puro, diseñado para Paco Roncero - uno de los chefs al filo de la cocina Española, quien respeta los fundamentos de la cocina española creando y experimentando con el alimento. La sensibilidad del chef hacia la nueva cocina sirvio como el punto de partida para el diseño de James & Mau. Esto creo un concepto que une la tradición con la innovación sin hacerse kitsch. El elemento clave fue un pasador, el objeto español popular que no ha sido olvidado en las tiendas de recuerdo de Madrid. 1,000 Pasadores fueron usados para crear una superficie retro iluminada que forma la cubierta de techo y una pared.

← View of wall and ceiling covered with 1,000 barrettes. Vista de la pared y techo cubiertos con 1,000 peinetas.

↑ View to bar. Vista hacia la barra.
← Exterior terrace. Terraza exterior.
↗ Interior view. Vista hacia el interior.
↘ Floor plan. Planta.
↘↘ Detail of barrettes. Detalle de peinetas.

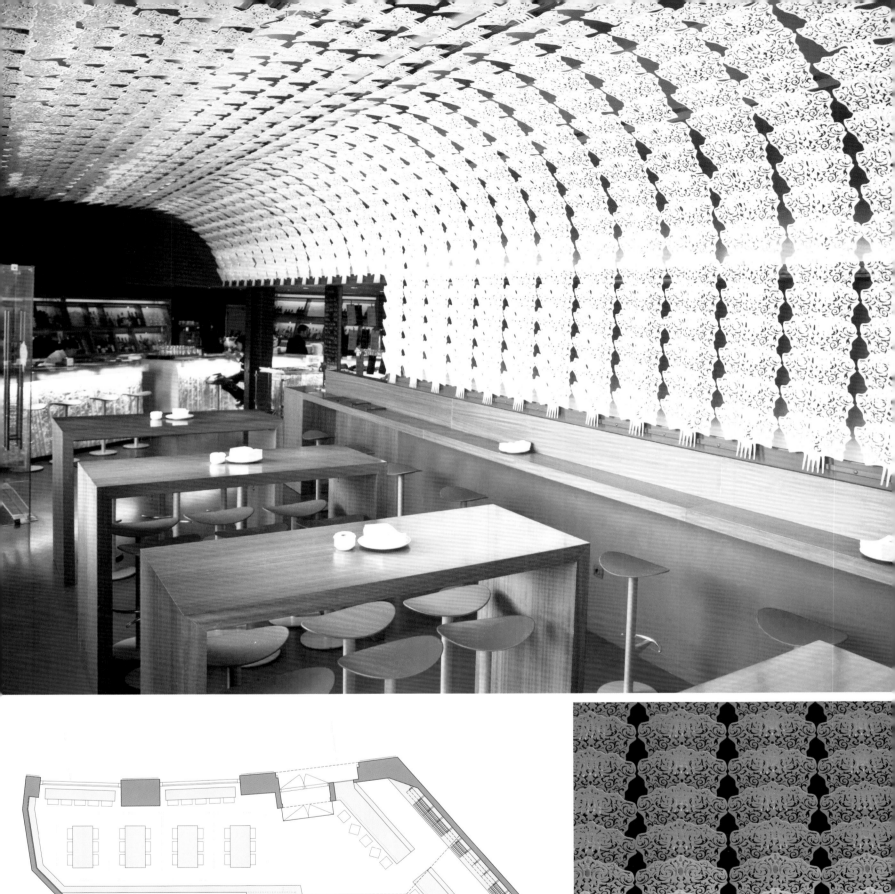

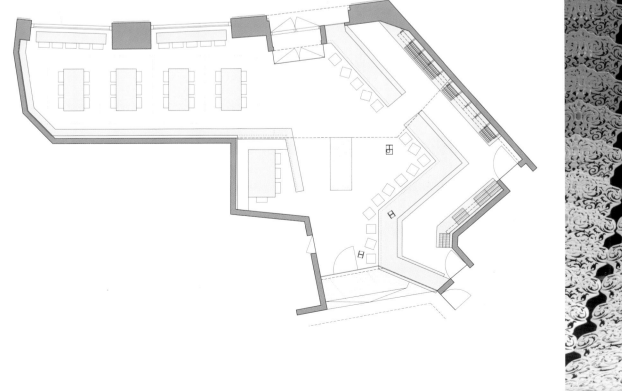

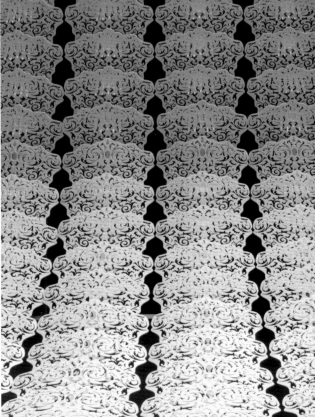

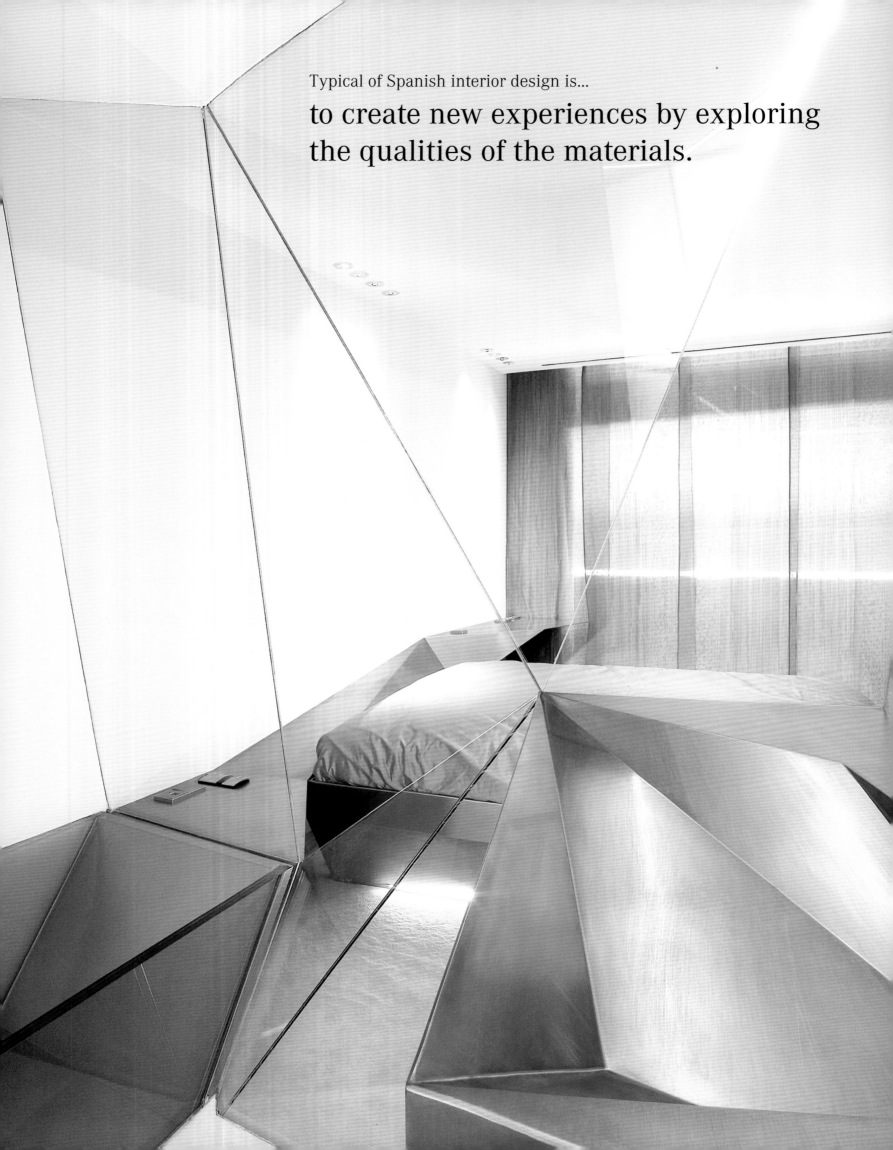

Typical of Spanish interior design is...

to create new experiences by exploring the qualities of the materials.

Hotel Puerta America, Level 4

Plasma Studio

Address: Avenida de América 41, 28002 Madrid. **Client:** Silken Hotels. **Completion:** 2004. **Main function:** Hotel, restaurant/bar. **Materials:** Stainless steel and glass.

This is sort of a science fiction space. The guest rooms and the hallway feature a big stainless steel surface and geometric forms similar to that of a spaceship. The fiction feeling is reinforced by a color gradient as an LED light seam that gradually changes and attempts to create a sensory tour, where only the intuition of the client counts. The same steel from the hallway gives shape to the shower, bath, headboard of the bed and the desk, which flow seemlesly in the same wall. Everything is a gigantic piece, which flows naturally in spite of the apparently aggressive shape it has. This is a young and dynamic space, which challenges the guest to touch and to discover every single corner.

Este es un espacio casi de ciencia-ficción. Tanto las habitaciones como el pasillo se resuelven con grandes piezas de acero inoxidable y formas geométricas que remiten a una nave espacial. La sensación de un proyecto de ficción está reforzada por un juego de luz de distintos colores, unas tiras de leds que refuerzan la intención de crear un recorrido sensorial, donde sólo manda la intuición del cliente. El mismo acero del pasillo da forma a la ducha, el baño, el cabecero de la cama y el escritorio, que discurren uno a continuación del otro organizados en la misma pared. Todo es una única y gigantesca pieza, que fluye con naturalidad pese a lo aparentemente agresivo de su forma. Éste es un espacio joven y dinámico, que reta al huésped a tocar y a descubrir cada esquina.

← View to bed from bathroom. Vista hacia la cama desde el baño.

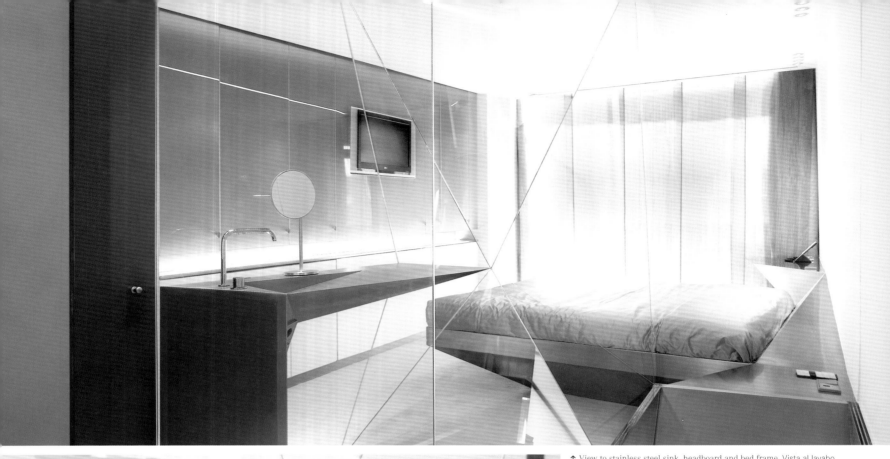

↑ View to stainless steel sink, headboard and bed frame. Vista al lavabo de acero inoxidable, cabecera y marco de la cama.
← Detail of sink. Detalle del lavabo.
↓ Room floor plan. Planta de habitación.
→ Interior perspective. Vista perspectiva del interior.

Typical of Spanish interior design is...
incorporating different cultures and tendencies.

Puro Hotel

Gabrielle Jangeby / DIS Inredning AB

Address: Montenegro 12, 07012 Palma de Mallorca. **Client:** Mats Wahlström. **Completion:** 2010, original: 18th century. **Building restoration:** Estudio de Arquitectura Álvaro Planchuelo. **Main function:** Hotel, restaurant, bar. **Materials:** Wood, mosaics, black slate and glass.

Puro Hotel is a former mansion turned into a modern, confident, genuine hotel, thought for the cosmopolitan and spiritual traveler. An urban oasis where the oriental spirit and the contemporary way of life intermingle with the Spanish history. With a mix of contemporary art by international artists like Peter Gröndahl, David Feucht and Kim Steeb, Puro's style has a sleeker contemporary feel to its public and private areas. The 51 guest rooms feature predominantly soft sand-colored hues with starker contrasts supplied by a dark wooden floor, silver cushions and an exquisite dresser (a modern rendition of a treasure chest). The combination of natural elements and contemporary art objects with sophisticated technology turns Puro into a special place to soothe body, mind and soul.

Puro Hotel es un antiguo palacete convertido en un hotel moderno, desenfadado, genuino, pensado para el viajero cosmopolita y espiritual. Un oasis urbano donde el espíritu oriental y el estilo de vida contemporáneo se entremezclan con la historia española. Con una mezcla de arte contemporánea por artistas internacionales como Peter Gröndahl, David Feucht y Kim Steeb, el estilo de Puro tiene un sentido más elegante y contemporáneo en sus áreas públicas y privadas. Las 51 habitaciones destacan matices suaves predominantemente de arena pintados con contrastes más fuertes suministrados por un piso oscuro de madera, cojines de plata y un tocador (una interpretación moderna de una caja de tesoro). La combinación de elementos naturales y objetos contemporáneos de arte con la tecnología sofisticada se convierte a Puro en un lugar especial para relajar el cuerpo, mente y alma.

← Junior Suite, Puro Joy. Suite Junior, Puro Joy.

↖ Opio Bar & Restaurant. Opio Bar y Restaurante.
↑ Interior patio. Patio interior.
← Lobby. Vestíbulo.
↗ Double bedroom, Puro Urbano. Habitación doble, Puro Urbano.
↓ First and second floor plan. Primera y segunda planta.
↘ Rooftop. Tejado.
↘↘ Entrance way. Entrada.

Typical of Spanish interior design is...

creating different moods throughout
the different spaces.

Restaurante El Merca'o

Vaíllo & Irigaray + Galar

Address: Calle Tafalla 5–7, 31002 Pamplona. **Client:** Nueva Hostelería del Mercado 2006 S.L. **Completion:** 2008. **Main function:** Restaurant, bar. **Materials:** 4,000 bottles of green glass, cauldrons lamps and acoustic ceilings, butcher's tables, benches and floors.

El Merca'o Restaurant occupies two floors: the first one connected with the market and the second one located in a semi-basement. There are two different ways of being: the daily one, opened, flexible, linked to street traffic and of the market itself, organizing the circulation and access across the bar; and a deeper, austere way, linked to the atmosphere with the concept of warehouse, underground (exposing the foundation of the own building in glass aquariums – showcases) and offering a quiet, serene and calmer place. The connection raised with the exterior stands out: street and market, this is generated across filters, a glass aquarium filled with bottles of green glass, which filters the light and the views.

El Restaurante El Merca'o ocupa dos plantas: la primera conectada con el mercado y la segunda ubicada en semi-sótano. Se ofrece también dos espacios, dos modos diferentes de estar: uno cotidiano, abierto, flexible, vinculado a las circulaciones de la calle y del propio mercado, organizando las circulaciones y accesos a través del bar; y otro más profundo, austero, vinculando su atmósfera con el concepto de bodega, de lugar bajo tierra (exponiendo la cimentación del propio edificio en acuarios-vitrina de vidrio) y ofreciendo un receptáculo reposado, sereno y más tranquilo. Destaca la conexión planteada con el exterior: calle y mercado, que se genera a través de filtros, en este caso, curiosamente, peceras de vidrio rellenas de botellas de vidrio verde, que filtran la luz y las vistas.

← View towards main façade from interior. Vista hacia la fachada principal desde el interior.

↖ Restrooms. Baños.
↑ Detail façade covered with green glass bottles. Detalle de la fachada cubierta con botellas de vidrio verde.
← Bar with view towards main façade. Barra con vista hacia la fachada principal.
↗ Dining area with pans as ceiling lamps. Comedor con lámparas de techo de cacerolas.
↘ Floor plans. Plantas.
↘↘ Lounge area. Lounge.

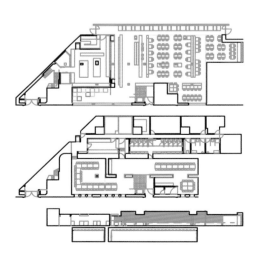

Typical of Spanish interior design is...
to intervene on the existing
to integrate into developing
a new space.

Hotel Moure

Ábalo Alonso Arquitectos

Address: Loureiros 6, 15702 Santiago de Compostela. **Client:** Liñares Bar. **Completion:** 2010. **Main function:** Hotel. **Materials:** Stone, wood, ceramic, glass and steel.

The renovation of this quiet hotel in Santiago de Compostela consists of a ramp at the main entrance, which welcomes the guests and takes them into an un-usual lobby, without a reception desk. The inner couryard perforates the building to illuminate and ventilate the interior. The layout of the guest rooms also breaks the typical room design, with the absence of doors in the bathrooms and the open-air bathtub.

La renovación de este hotel tranquilo en Santiago de Compostela consiste en una rampa en la entrada principal, que da la bienvenida a los invitados y los toma en un vestíbulo insólito, sin un escritorio de recepción. El patio interior perfora el edificio para iluminar y ventilar el interior. La disposición de las habitaciones de huéspedes también rompe el diseño de espacio típico, con la ausencia de puertas en los cuartos de baño y la bañera al aire libre.

← Guest room. Habitación.

↖ Guest room with outdoor bathtub. Habitación con bañera exterior.
↑ Upward view from interior courtyard. Vista hacia arriba desde el patio interior.
← Staircase. Escalera.
↗ View towards bathtub. Vista hacia la bañera.
↘ Typical guest room floor plan. Planta tipica de habitaciones.
↘↘ Living area. Sala de estar.

Typical of Spanish interior design is...

to provoke to imagine and dream in a typical Sevillan space.

Hospes las Casas del Rey de Baeza

Hospes Design

Address: Calle Santiago 2, 41003 Sevilla. **Client:** Hospes. **Completion:** 2010. **Main function:** Hotel, spa, restaurant/bar. **Materials:** Ceramics, seagrass and stone.

This enclave of typically Sevillian architecture was a neighborhood patio in the 18th century. Nowadays, it is the perfect scenery to free your imagination and let yourself go. Its 41 rooms allow guests to discover the decorated places with columns, ceramics, seagrass and stone, earthenware pitchers and traditional works of art, together with colonial style furniture in a fresh and friendly ambience.

Este bello enclave de arquitectura típicamente sevillana que fue patio de vecinos en el siglo XVIII, es hoy el marco perfecto para que los huéspedes de Hospes en Sevilla encuentren el sosiego reparador que incita a imaginar y soñar. Sus 41 estancias permiten al huésped descubrir rincones con columnas, cerámicas, botijos y elementos de otras épocas, en combinación con un mobiliario de estilo colonial.

← Interior courtyard. Patio interior.

↖ Deluxe guest room. Habitación Deluxe.
↑ View into interior courtyard from rooftop. Vista del patio interior desde el tejado.
← Senzone Restauant. Restaurante Senzone.
↗ Junior Suite. Suite Junior.
↘ Senzone Pool Bar. Bar con Piscina Senzone.
↘↘ Bathroom. Baño.

Typical of Spanish interior design is...
to respect the existing and
integrate harmony and function.

Lapiaz

Stone Designs

Address: Cerro Javalambre 1, Camarena de la Sierra. **Client:** Grupo Aramon. **Completion:** 2009. **Building architect:** José María Galve. **Main function:** Restaurant. **Materials:** Wood, wool textile and lacquer metal.

Stone Designs captures the simplicity and naturalness of the environment in their most recent project Lapiaz Restaurant, through the use of custom wood furniture accented with bright colors, exposed columns and beams, and painted mural tree trunks. This self-service restaurant and a chocolateria within the main Javalambre Ski Resort building in Teruel by architect José María Galve. The architects were asked to respond to the existing bold resort building, characterised by its large glass façade looking out on to the ski runs and the surrounding forest. The concept developed around two core themes, the first being respect for the building's architecture, which Stone Designs wanted to take maximum advantage of, strengthening its identity with their interior design proposal. Secondly, the interior design was used to merge the external and internal environment by treating the interior as a real landscape. A forest of timber clad columns and cylindrical lights form the backdrop of the restaurant.

Stone Designs captura la simplicidad y la naturalidad del ambiente en su proyecto más reciente, el restaurante Lapiaz, con el uso de muebles de encargo de madera acentuados con colores brillantes, columnas expuestas, vigas, y troncos de árbol de mural pintados. Este restaurante de autoservicio y chocolateria esta ubicado dentro del edificio de Estación de esquí principal Javalambre en Teruel, diseñado por el arquitecto José María Galve. Los arquitectos tenian que responder al edificio existente valiente, caracterizado por su fachada de cristal grande con vistas hacia las pistas de esquí y el bosque circundante. El concepto fue desarrollado alrededor de dos temas principales, el primero consistio en respetar la arquitectura del edificio, de la cual Stone Designs quiso tomar la maxima ventaja para reforzar su identidad con su oferta de diseño interior. En segundo lugar, el diseño interior fue usado para combinar el ambiente externo e interno tratando el interior como un verdadero paisaje. Un bosque de columnas revestidas de madera y luces cilíndricas forman el telón del restaurante.

← Ground floor, main dining room and viewing-point from façade. Planta baja, comedor principal y mirador de fachada.

↑ Second floor, café with hot chocolate. Segunda planta, chocolatería.
← Ground floor, staircase and café with hot chocolate. Planta baja,
escalera y chocolatería.
↓ Ground floor plan. Planta baja.
↗ Ground floor with aerial view. Planta baja vista aéria

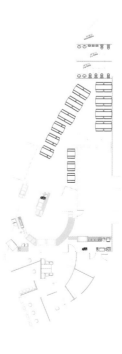

Typical of Spanish interior design is...
using the past to create the future.

Arrop Restaurant

Francesc Rifé

Address: Calle Almirante 14, 46003 Valencia. **Completion:** 2009. **Main function:** Restaurant. **Materials:** Wood, glass, stone and metal.

The restaurant of a Michelin star, directed by Ricard Camarena, sits beneath the grand Hotel Palacio Marqués de Caro, the first hotel – monument of Valencia. The design integrates and respects the evidences of the history of this building, which are combined by the talent and the details of a timeless vision: noble stones, noble woods and integration, glass and metal; a great fragment of the Arabic wall of the city has emerged from between the rubbles and has given to the restaurant a prominent role. As if it would forebode, this former strength integrated with success in the sleek design which marks perfectly the aim of Arrop's kitchen: to rescue the ancient and to embellish it with a touch of discreet modernity.

El restaurante de una estrella Michelin, dirigido por Ricard Camarena se encuentra ubicado en la planta baja de un edificio histórico que alberga El Hotel Palacio Marqués de Caro, el primer hotel-monumento de Valencia. El diseño integra y respeta las evidencias de la historia viva de este inmueble, que se combinan con el talento y los detalles de una vision atemporal: piedras nobles, maderas nobles e integradoras, vidrio y metal; un gran fragmento de la muralla árabe de la ciudad ha emergido de entre los escombros y ha dado al restaurante un mayor protagonismo aún. Como si fuera un presagio, esa antigua fortaleza, integrada con mucho acierto en el vistoso diseño de la sala, marca perfectamente el objetivo de la cocina de Arrop: rescatar lo antiguo y embellecerlo con un toque de discreta modernidad.

← Lounge. Lounge.

↖ Private dining area. Comedor en zona privada.
↑ Living room. Sala de estar.
← Main dining area. Comedor principal.
→ Exposed stone on ground and wall. Piedra expuesta en piso y pared.

Typical of Spanish interior design is...

to follow sinuous lines to create a fluid space.

Hotel Puerta America, Level 1

Zaha Hadid Architects

Address: Avenida de América 41, 28002 Madrid. **Client:** Silken Hotels. **Completion:** 2004. **Main function:** Hotel, restaurant/bar. **Materials:** LG Hi-Macs (white acrylic).

Hotel Puerta America offers twelve different aesthetic experiences to choose from by twelve renowned architects. The first floor of the hotel features Zaha Hadid's all-white, thermoformed Corian cave, a dream world — walls, floor, and ceiling flowing seamlessly into one another with only soft gradients of light and shadow to distinguish each new surface. Every single element with its LED signs, sliding door to the bathroom, bathtub and vanity unit, bed, shelves, chair and a cantilevered bench by the window which doubles up as a table — is rounded in a single curved sweep. A further unique element of this suite of bedrooms is the use of color. Customers can opt for an alpine white or a black bedroom, or even choose a white bedroom with a black bathroom, black bedroom and white bathroom or a black bedroom and an orange bathroom.

El Hotel Puerta América ofrece 12 experiencias diferentes estéticas a escoger por 12 arquitectos renombrados. La primera planta del hotel destaca a Zaha Hadid todo-blanco, la cueva en termoformado Corian, un mundo de ensueño - paredes, piso, y el techo fluyen a la perfección el uno en el otro con los gradientes suaves de luz y sombra para distinguir cada nueva superficie. Cada elemento con sus LED signs, deslizando la puerta al cuarto de baño, la bañera y la unidad de vanidad, la cama, estantería, la silla y un banco voladizo por la ventana que se dobla para convertirse en una mesa - se acopla a las formas sinuosas del espacio. Un elemento remoto de estas suites es el empleo de color. Los clientes pueden optar por las habitaciones de alpino blanco o una habitación negra, o aún escoger una habitación blanca con un baño negro, habitación negra y el baño blanco o un habitación negra y baño naranja.

← Bathroom, toilet design from Stefano Giovannoni for Alessi. Baño, inodoro diseñado por Stefano Giovannoni para Alessi.

↑ Interior with futuristic lines. Interior con líneas futuristas.
← Bathroom with orange lighting. Baño Iluminado de naranja.
↗ Hallway features LG Hi-Macs (acrylic material). Pasillo destaca LG Hi-Macs (material acrílico).
↘ Perspective drawing. Dibujo de la perspectiva.
↘↘ Illuminated hallway. Pasillo iluminado.

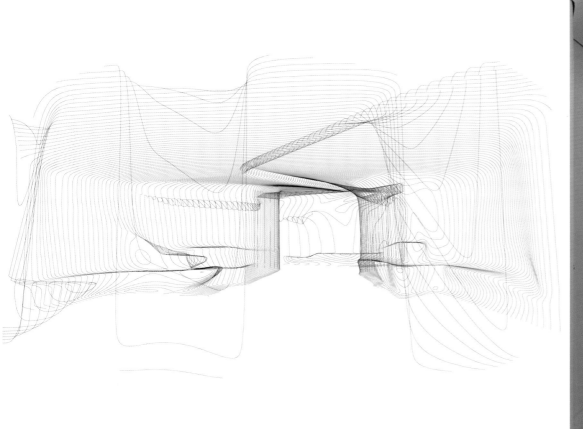

culture & leisure

Typical of Spanish interior design is...

creating an interconnection between
existing and new elements

Cultural Center and New Town Hall of Archidona

Ramón Fernández-Alonso

Location: Archidona, Málaga. **Client:** Obispado de Alcalá de Henares. **Completion:** 2010. **Main function:** Cultural center and town hall.
Materials: Glass, wood and black basaltina stone.

The intervention departs from a double analysis: on the one hand the historical side of a typical building of a period of time and an important element, such as the Plaza Ochavada, and on the other hand, the required typology of a Cultural Center and Town hall. The design consisted in preserving and recovering as much as possible from the 18th century building, which would house the representative areas and mayor's office. Furthermore, a new building had to be designed to house the rest of the program: cultural center, in the lower levels and offices in the upper levels. Also an independent volume was created, a prism "carved" in glass featuring a "glass curtain" to control the light in the offices, allowing views to the landscape, and finding a transition between the new building and the former one, concealing the line of intersection of its respective façade planes.

La intervención parte de un doble análisis: por un lado el histórico de un edificio característico de una época y elemento configurador de una pieza de mayor orden como es la Plaza Ochavada, y por otro, el tipológico que demanda el uso último al que se somete como Centro Cultural y Ayuntamiento. El diseño consistio en preservar y recuperar en lo posible el edificio del siglo XVIII, donde se ubicará las áreas representativas y Alcaldía. Y en la creación de un nuevo edificio que alojará el resto de funciones: centro cultural, en plantas inferiores y oficinas en las superiores. Asi mismo se proyecto un volumen de marcada independencia en configuración y materiales, un prisma "tallado" en vidrio que establece a manera de una "cortina de vidrio" el control de la luz, en las oficinas, permitiendo ver el paisaje, y resolviendo de forma sencilla la transición entre el edificio nuevo y el antiguo, ocultando la línea de intersección de sus respectivos planos de fachada.

← Interior with vaulted ceiling. Interior con techo abovedado.

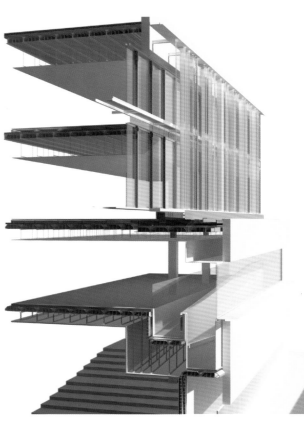

↖ Ramps with open views to surroundings. Rampas con vistas abiertas al entorno.

↑ Sectional detail. Detalle de corte.

← Stairs leading to offices. Escaleras hacia las oficinas.

↓ Second and third floor plan. Segunda y tercera planta.

↗ Hallway with view to angled façade. Pasillo con vista hacia la fachada angulada.

↘ Panoramic view from ramp. Vista panoramica desde la rampa.

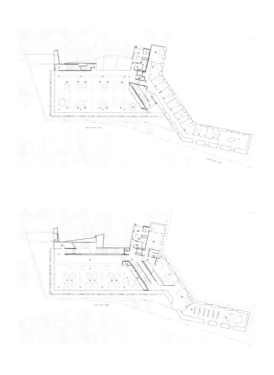

Typical of Spanish interior design is...

finding a connection between new and existing elements.

Baños Arabes Aire de Barcelona

Alonso Balaguer y Arquitectos Asociados

Address: Paseo Picasso 22, 08003 Barcelona. **Client:** Baños Aires Grupo Aires S.L. **Completion:** 2008. **Main function:** Spa. **Materials:** Black granite, marble macael and brick and stone.

The Arab baths are located in a renovated warehouse with stone arches that now provide a wonderful setting for "hammam" salt water floating baths, cold plunge pools, jacuzzi, saunas and steam rooms. The functional program develops in three levels (water zones, relaxation zones and hammam in the basement, reception and dressing rooms in the ground floor, massage cabins and vichy showers in the mezzanine floor). The design style and simplicity of the selected materials (black granite, marble macael, brick and stone) characterize this intervention. The smelting columns and the bordered girders create a dialogue with the new volumes to give a new appearance to the Andalusian courtyard; the solemnity of the former tunnel vaults of the water zone are illuminated in a dramatic way to balance with the continuity of the marble that constitutes the pavement, covers the swimming pools and creates the seats and the plinth.

Los baños árabes estan ubicados¬ en un depósito renovado con arcos de piedra que ahora proporciona un maravilloso ajuste para el agua salada "hamman" baños flotantes, fondos de zambullida fríos, Jacuzzi, saunas y baños de vapor. El programa funcional se desarrolla en tres niveles (zona de aguas, zonas de relax y hamman en la planta sótano, recepción y vestuarios en la planta baja, cabinas de masajes y duchas de vichy en la planta entresuelo). El rigor estilístico constante y la sencillez de los materiales adoptados (granito negro, mármol macael, ladrillo y piedra) caracterizan esta intervención. A la textura de la obra vista se contrapone la superficie de los cristales apenas tamizados por gasas ligeras; las columnas de fundición y las vigas ribeteadas dialogan con los volúmenes nuevos enseñando una relectura del patio andaluz; la solemnidad de las antiguas bóvedas de cañón de la zona de aguas, iluminadas de forma dramática, se equilibra con la continuidad del mármol que constituye el pavimento, recubre las piscinas y forma los asientos y los zócalos.

← Warm swimming pool. Piscina templada.

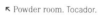

↖ Powder room. Tocador.
↑ Bowls. Cuencos.
← Access to salt-water swimming pool. Acceso a piscina agua salada.
↗ Warm and hot swimming pool. Piscina templada y caliente.
↘ Lobby. Vestíbulo.
↘↘ Dressing room. Vestidores.

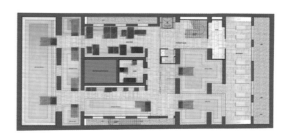

Typical of Spanish interior design is...

the historical relationship between
architecture and water.

Water Museum in Lanjarón

Juan Domingo Santos

Location: Lanjarón. **Client:** Obispado de Alcalá de Henares. **Completion:** 2010. **Main function:** Museum. **Materials:** Finnish fir wood panels and stone walls.

This former flourmill and distillery building now houses the Water Museum, a small-scaled display of the relationship of Lanjarón with water. There are three rooms, in the first one an audivisual show explains the water's cycles. The second room is an audiovisual space that explains the aspects of water related with the agriculture, health, and industry. The third room is dedicated to the historic aspects related with the water of Lanjarón. The small exposition is quite appropriately situated next to the Río Lanjarón. At the other side of the river a path goes up into the mountains as an invitation to experience aspects of water in its natural surroundings.

Este antiguo molino de harina y destilería ahora aloja el Museo de Agua, una pequeña demostración sobre la relación de Lanjarón con el agua. Hay tres espacios, el primero una sala de audivisual explica los ciclos del agua. El segundo espacio es una sala de audivisual que explica los aspectos del agua relacionada con la agricultura, la salud, y la industria. El tercer espacio esta dedicado a los aspectos históricos relacionados con el agua de Lanjarón. Esta pequeña exposición esta muy bien ubicada al lado del Río Lanjarón. Al otro lado del río un camino sube a las montañas como una invitación para experimentar los aspectos del agua en su entorno natural.

← Pavilion hovering over pool marks the museum's entrance. El pabellón que se cierne sobre el fondo marca la entrada del museo.

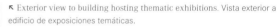
↖ Exterior view to building hosting thematic exhibitions. Vista exterior a edificio de exposiciones temáticas.
↑ Entrance pavilion. Pabellón de entrada.
← Glass panel employed for visual projections. Panel de cristal empleado para proyecciones visuales.

Typical of Spanish interior design is...

expressionist and contrastive.

Rivas Vaciamadrid Parish Center

Vicens + Ramos

Address: Calle de Los Nibelungos, 28523 Madrid. **Client:** Obispado de Alcalá de Henares. **Completion:** 2008. **Main function:** Church, Parish offices and priest housing. **Materials:** Steel porticos and reinforced concrete.

The complex is made up of two independent buildings: one houses the church and the chapel, in a structure with large steel porticos, while a second volume with a structure of reinforced concrete accommodates the housing and parochial rooms. Both are tied together by a continuous corten steel skin which, as a whole, creates a piece that gives an image of great unity and rotundity. The northern and southern façades are symmetrical except in the building of parochial spaces, where on the northern face, the steel skin curves to form the main access to the nave.

El complejo está compuesto de dos edificios independientes: la iglesia y la capilla, en una estructura con pórticos grandes de acero, mientras un segundo volumen con una estructura de hormigón armado le da alojamiento a los espacios de vivienda y parroquiales. Ambos estan unidos por una superficie continua de acero de corten que al final le da una imagen de gran unidad y corpulencia. Las fachadas del norte y sur son simétricas, a excepcion de la fachada del edificio con los servicios parroquiales, en la cual la fachada del norte, la superficie de acero se encurva para formar el acceso principal hacia la nave.

← The nave. La nave.

←← Daily chapel. Capilla de diario.
↙↙ The nave and altar. La nave y el altar.
↙↙ The Baptistery. El Baptisterio.
← Altar. Altar.
↑ Elevation and watercolor sketch. Elevación y bosquejo de acuarela.
↙ Floor plans. Plantas.
↓ Exterior view. Vista exterior.

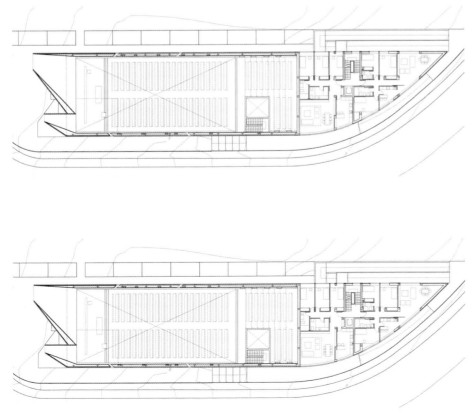

Typical of Spanish interior design is...
the use of new techniques to create
a new and harmonious unity.

Cultural Center Lavapiés

José Ignacio Linazasoro Rodríguez

Address: Calles Mesón de Paredes / Sombrerete, 28012 Madrid. **Completion:** 2004. **Main function:** Auditorium and meeting rooms. **Materials:** Stone, wood and red bricks.

The ruins of the old church located in Lavapiés, one of the oldest quarters of Madrid, have been repurposed for a library, and a new building has been built which consists of an auditorium and meeting rooms. In the interior, the old brick walls have been preserved and restored with stone and wood. Light penetrates deep into the buildings, and this is stressed in particularly by the shaft of light between the old building and the new one highlighting a concrete staircase. The project illustrates how continuity and ruptures in history, techniques and aesthetics can create a new and harmonious unity.

Las ruinas de la antigua iglesia localizada en Lavapiés, uno de los barrios más viejos de Madrid, ha recobrado vida con una biblioteca; y un edificio nuevo ha sido construido para alojar un auditorio y salas de conferencias. En el interior las paredes viejas de ladrillos rojos han sido conservadas y restauradas con piedra y madera. La luz penetra profundamente el interior, a traves de la claraboya entre el edificio existente y el nuevo, el cual destaca una escalera de concreto. El proyecto demuestra como la continuidad y ruptura en la historia, técnicas y la estética puede crear una unidad nueva y armoniosa.

← Upward view towards vault. Vista hacia la bóveda.

↖ Shaft of light between the old building and the new one highlighting a concrete staircase. Eje de luz entre el edificio existente y el nuevo destacando una escalera de concreto.

↑ Interior view. Vista interna.

← Detail concrete staircase. Detalle de escalera de concreto.

↗ Library, reading area. Biblioteca, zona de lectura.

↘ First floor plan. Primera planta.

↘↘ Detail ceiling. Detalle del techo.

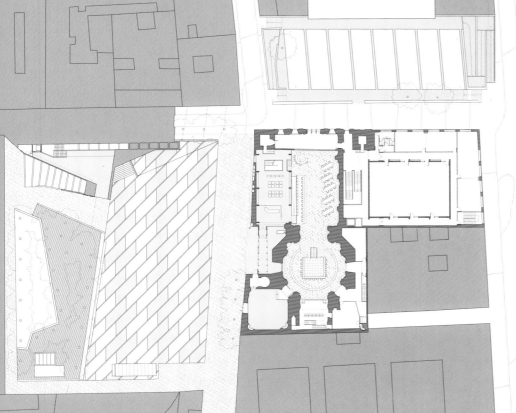

Typical of Spanish interior design is...

to give a sense of floating in space through the use of light materials.

Nursery School in Pamplona

Javier Larraz

Address: Parcela E.1.1 - Buztintxury, 31002 Pamplona. **Completion:** 2009. **Main function:** Kindergarten. **Materials:** Concrete, glass and rubber.

The building is organized as a series of four parallel bodies in which fully built and empty areas are alternated. A body with administration services is located at the west of the site and filters the traffic noise from this side. The empty central space is illuminated through a skylight that emerges above the rest of the building and a third body houses the children's areas, including classrooms, workshops, refectories and bedrooms. Lastly, the external backyard is conceived as a prolongation of the classroom spaces through the opening of large windows. Diverse colors and textures (concrete, rubber and grass) create suggestive and varied playing spaces for the children.

El edificio esta organizado como una serie de cuatro volumenes paralelos en los cuales hay zonas totalmente construidas y las zonas vacías son alternadas. Un volumen con servicios de administración esta localizado en el lado oeste del emplazamiento y filtra el ruido de tráfico de ese lado. El espacio central vacío esta iluminado por una claraboya que nace en la parte superior del resto del edificio; y el tercer volumen aloja el area de juegos de niños, incluyendo aulas, talleres, refectorios y habitaciones para dormir. Por ultimo, el patio trasero externo es concebido como una prolongación de los espacios de aula por la apertura de ventanas grandes. Colores diversos y texturas (el hormigón, el caucho y el césped) crean espacios de juego sugestivos y variados para los niños.

← Hallway with view towards playroom. Pasillo con vista hacia la sala de juegos.

↑ Entrance pavilion. Pabellón de entrada.
← View to playroom through glass. Vista hacia la sala de juegos a traves del cristal.
↗ View towards playground from interior. Vista hacia patio desde el interior.
↘ Floor plan. Planta.
↘↘ Exterior view. Vista del exterior.

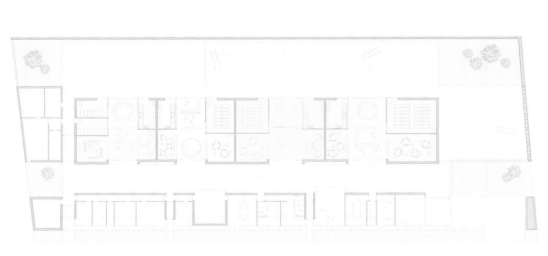

home & liv

ing

Typical of Spanish interior design is...

to give honest respect to history.

Interior with a History in The Gothic

Agnés Blanch y Elina Vila / MINIM

Address: Carrer de la Junta de Comerç 19, 08001 Barcelona. **Completion:** 2009, original: 19th century. **Main function:** Living. **Materials:** Wood, pine Douglas floor.

The basis of this project was truly exceptional: a housing incorporating an ancient 500 years old cloister with an intervention by Antoni Gaudí. Facing a similar challenge, the designers applied their project philosophy with the utmost rigor and restored and rehabilitated each of the original architectural elements. It is a modern restoration with and honest respect to history.

La base de este proyecto fue realmente excepcional: un alojamiento que incorpora un claustro antiguo de 500 años con una intervención por Antoni Gaudí. Afrontando un desafío similar, los diseñadores aplicaron su filosofía de proyecto con el rigor extremo y restauraron y rehabilitaron cada uno de los elementos originales arquitectónicos. Esto es una restauración moderna con y el respeto honesto a la historia.

← Living room. Salón.

↖ Bedroom. Habitación.
↑ Detail exterior. Detalle del exterior.
← Dining/living. Comedor/salón.
↓ Floor plan. Planta.
→ Living room with vaulted ceilings. Salón con techo abovedado.

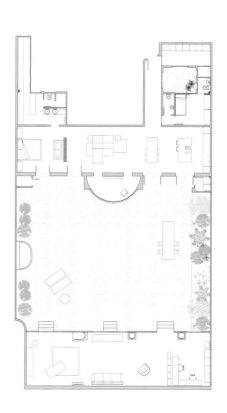

Typical of Spanish interior design is...

the overlapping between the 19th century and contemporary design.

Casa Alibei

Habitan Arquitectos

Address: Calle Ali Bei 98, Pral 2, 08013 Barcelona. **Client:** Yoel Karaso & Cecilia Tham. **Completion:** 2005, original: 1894. **Main function:** Living. **Materials:** Birch wood, slate stone, original mosaics and metallic trays.

This apartment is placed in a 1894 building of the Eixample neighborhood of Barcelona, affected by an urban development plan of the city hall, which means that at any time it can be expropriated. Departing from this hypothesis, the renovation was based on the concept of "take away": the new elements, like the kitchen and bathroom, were designed to be fitted into any walls; they are more like furniture. So, in case of eviction they can be taken with. The canny renovation strategy honored the dazzling turn-of-the-century tile work and ornate moldings. The result is an overlapping between the design, color and baroque of the end of the 19th century and contemporary minimalist design.

Este piso está situado en un bloque de 1894 del Eixample de Barcelona, afectado por un plan urbanístico de ayuntamiento, lo que significa que en cualquier momento puede ser expropiado. Partiendo de esta hipótesis, el proyecto de reforma se baso en el concepto de " Take away": los elementos nuevos, como cocina y baño, fueron pensados como muebles de madera exentos que pudieran ser recuperados en caso de desalojo. La estrategia de renovación astuta honró el trabajo de azulejo deslumbrante existente y los moldeados adornados. El resultado es una superposición entre el diseño, colorido y barroco de finales del siglo XIX y diseño contemporáneo minimalista.

← Kitchen with original floor tiling. Cocina con pisos originales.

↖ Dining room. Comedor.
↑ Hallway. Pasillo.
← Freestanding bathtub and sink unit out of plywood and slate. Módulo de bañera con fregadero aislada de madera contrachapada y pizarra.
↓ Floor plan. Planta.
↗ View to living room from kitchen. Vista hacia el salón desde la cocina.
↘ Children's room. Habitación de niños.
↘↘ Shower. Ducha.

Typical of Spanish interior design is...
luxury, comfort, design
and quality.

Interiorismo Viviendas en Serrano

A-cero

Address: Calle Serrano, Madrid. **Completion:** 2010. **Main function:** Home. **Materials:** Silk wallpaper, exotic woods.

Luxury, comfort, design and quality have been joined in eight new flats. Each one of the flats has a different distribution, but they all have large windows and skylights in lounges, dining rooms and hallways. Furthermore, white walls and roofs increase clarity, cleanliness and warmth in the interior. All flats have ample spaces and a functional distribution based on diaphanous rooms, double height roofs and a practical and effective distribution. Floors are made of different materials: travertine marble, wood and porcelánico dark gray (in kitchens and bathrooms). The furniture (designed by A-cero) is gray, black or white and has clean and modern lines.

El lujo, la comodidad, el diseño y la calidad han sido unidos en ocho pisos nuevos. Cada uno de los pisos tiene una distribución diferente, pero todos tienen ventanas grandes y claraboyas en los salones, comedores y vestíbulos. Además, las paredes blancas y azoteas aumentan la claridad, la limpieza y sensaciones de calidez en el interior. Todos los pisos tienen espacios amplios y una distribución funcional basada en espacios diáfanos, azoteas de doble altura y una distribución práctica y eficaz. Los pisos son hechos de materiales diferentes: mármol travertino, madera y color gris oscuro porcelánico (en cocinas y baños). Los muebles (diseñados por A-cero) son grises, negros o blancos y tienen líneas definidas y modernas.

← Living room. Sala de estar.

↖ Interior view. Vista interna.
← Bathroom. Baño.
↗ Bedroom. Habitación.
↘ Kitchen. Cocina.
↘↘ Desk. Escritorio.

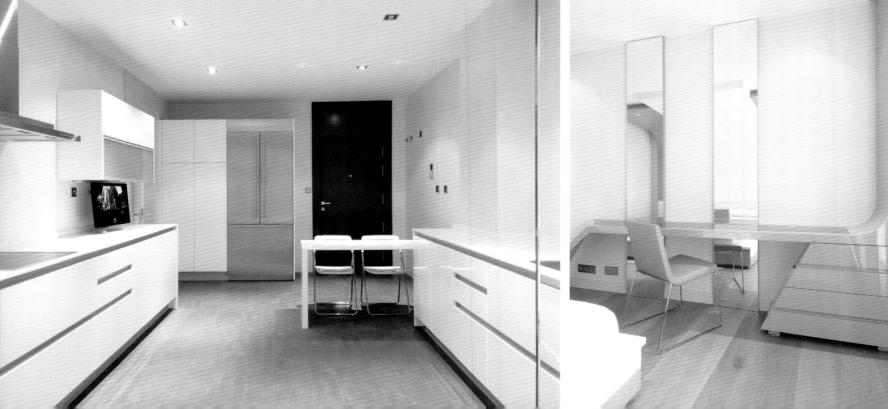

Typical of Spanish interior design is...

to create a bridge between the past and the present.

Santpere47

Miel Arquitectos

Address: Ronda de Sant Pere 47, Principal 1ª, 08010 Barcelona. **Client:** Miguel Angel Borras & Elodie Grammont. **Completion:** 2008. **Main function:** Living. **Materials:** Wood, steel and ceramic.

Santpere47, the open-plan interior features a staircase with mirrored glass on the risers, creating reflections of the carpeted treads. Recesses in the walls and stairs plus a mezzanine floor provide storage space. Two golden strips divide the apartment diagonally above head-height, forming coat hooks, a wine rack and supporting a ladder to the mezzanine along the way. The alteration of the flat Santpere47 is a re-reading of the spatial structure of a typical apartment of the end of the 19th century, succession of isolated rooms and disconnected courts. Santpere47 dissolves the structure of walls through new physical and visual connections.

Santpere47, la planta abierta del interior destaca una escalera con el cristal reflejado sobre las contrahuellas, creando las reflexiones de las alfombradas pisadas. Huecos en las paredes y la escalera más en el piso de entresuelo proporcionan almacenaje en el espacio. Dos tiras de oro dividen el apartamento en diagonal encima de la altura delantera, formando percheros para colgar los abrigos, un estante de vino y apoyando una escalera al entresuelo a lo largo del camino. La alteración del piso de Santpere47 es un releer de la estructura espacial del típico piso del fines del siglo XIX, la sucesión de espacios aislados y tribunales deshilvanados. Santpere47 desvanece la estructura de paredes a traves de nuevas conexiones físicas y visuales.

← Dining/living room. Comedor/sala de estar.

↖ Main bedroom. Habitación principal.
↑ Staircase with original mosaics. Escalera con mosaicos originales.
← View to coat rack and hallway. Vista hacia el perchero y pasillo.
↓ Floor plans. Plantas.
↗ Interior with double-height ceilings. Interior con techos de altura doble.
↘ View to bookshelf from kitchen. Vista a estantería desde la cocina.
↘↘ Detail staircase. Detalle de la escalera.

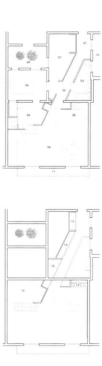

Typical of Spanish interior design is...

clear and radical concepts in the
creation and distribution of spaces.

Vivienda en el Barrio Gótico

YLAB arquitectos

Location: Barcelona. **Client:** Mr. Hellyer. **Completion:** 2010. **Main function:** Living. **Materials:** Pine wood, anodized aluminum and marfil lacquer.

The project consists of a renovation of a house placed in the heart of the Barrio Gótico neighborhood of Barcelona, behind the Town hall. Composed by a sequence of wide and bright rooms communicating between hollow spaces with archs, it supports the ceilings with wooden girders and vaults or the exterior carpentries of wood with shutters. The client wanted to reform the space to turn it into a modern and functional house where the traditional elements were coexisting with the new design without turning out to be predominant. The renovation project is based on the reintepretation of the spatial existing structure of the different rooms and uses, endowing the spaces with new designs and functions and creating new connections between them. The result is a contemporary house of very definite and different environments, with visual unexpected connections and where the original structure contributes to the depth and beauty.

El proyecto consiste en la reforma de una vivienda situada en el corazón del Barrio Gótico de Barcelona, tras el Ayuntamiento. Compuesto por una secuencia de salas amplias y luminosas comunicadas entre sí por huecos de paso con arco, mantiene los techos con vigas de madera y arcos de bovedilla o las carpinterías exteriores de madera con contraventanas. Su propietario deseaba reformar el espacio para convertirlo en una vivienda moderna y funcional donde los elementos tradicionales convivieran con el nuevo diseño sin resultar predominantes. El proyecto de reforma se basa en la reinterpretación de la estructura espacial existente de salas distintas con usos y ambientes diferenciados, dotando los espacios de nuevos diseños y funciones y creando nuevas conexiones entre ellos. El resultado es una vivienda contemporánea de ambientes muy definidos y distintos entre sí, con conexiones visuales inesperadas y donde la estructura original aporta profundidad y belleza al conjunto.

← Dining room. Comedor.

↖ Kitchen with walls covered in pine wood. Cocina con paredes recubiertas en madera de pino.
↑ Interior courtyard. Patio interior.
← View to kitchen and dining room from hallway. Vista hacia la cocina y comedor desde el pasillo.
↓ Floor plan. Planta
↗ Bathroom. Baño.
↘ Kitchen/dining room. Cocina/comedor.
↘↘ View to bathroom from hallway. Vista hacia el baño desde el pasillo.

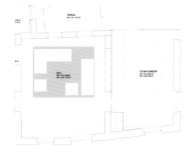

Typical of Spanish interior design is...
the interplay between light
and silhouettes.

Prefab House

mycc oficina de arquitectura

Location: Cadeira, Coruña. **Completion:** 2009. **Main function:** Living. **Materials:** Cement and wood fibre (walls and roof) and corten steel (gabled ends).

Constructed off-site using beams and galvanized steel columns for the frame; this prefab was transported by truck to the site and assembled in just three days. The design was inspired by the surrounding pitched roof farmhouses and abundant eucalyptus forests that pepper the steep hillside encompassing the site. The house comprises six modules: two contain the bathroom, stairs and kitchen, three provide living areas and the last a bedroom with a moveable partition wall. The roof and perimeter walls are clad with Viroc®, a prefabricated mixture of cement and wood shavings, which is characteristically strong, lightweight and echoes the colors of the eucalyptus forests nearby.

Esta casa prefabricada fue transportada al emplazamiento y montado en solo tres días. El diseño fue inspirado por las casas de labranza del entorno con tejado a dos aguas y los bosques de eucalipto abundantes que acribillan la ladera escarpada que abarca el emplazamiento. La casa esta compuesta de seis módulos: dos albergan el baño, la escalera y la cocina, tres proporcionan áreas para estar y el último una habitación con una pared móvil de partición. La azotea y las paredes del perímetro estan vestidas con Viroc ®, una mezcla prefabricada de cemento y virutas, que son característicamente fuertes, de peso ligero y ue repiten los colores de los bosques de eucalipto del entorno.

← Living room with double-height ceilings and "Fire-Orb". Salón con techos de altura doble y una chimenea "Fire-Orb".

↑ Interior, second floor. Interior, segunda planta.
← Interior view through open façade. Vista interna a través de la fachada abierta.
↓ First floor plan. Primera planta.
→ View to living room from second floor. Vista al salón desde la segunda planta.
↘ View of front façade by night. Vista de la fachada principal de noche.

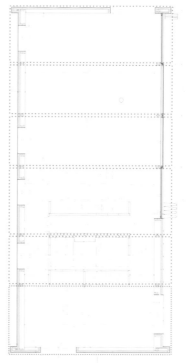

Typical of Spanish interior design is...
minimalism gives tranquility.

Marquesa 11–13 Housing Reform

José Antonio Molia Saiz + Marià Castelló Martínez

Address: Carrer de la Marquesa de Villalonga 11, 08017 Barcelona. **Completion:** 2010. **Main function:** Home. **Materials:** Pre-existing solid wood pine floor properly restored, plaster coating in the partitions, ceilings and walls, synthetic quartz plates in white and transparent laminated glass for the bathrooms.

In order to achieve greater harmony and homogenize the original surface with the new one, a limited palette of essential material were used, such as the pre-existing solid pine wood floor was properly restored, plaster coating in the partitions, ceilings and vertical walls. Water-resistant an MDF board was painted in white for furniture. Synthetic quartz plates in white and transparent laminated glass for the bathrooms and exposed concrete in the pillars of the existing vertical structure.

Con el objetivo de lograr una mayor armonía y homogeneizar el sustrato original con la obra nueva, se ha utilizado una reducida paleta de materiales que, fundamentalmente, son un pavimiento preexistente de madera meciza de pino debidamente restaurado. Revestimientos de yeso en tabiquería, techos y resto de cerramientos verticales. Tablero de DM Hidrófugo lacado en blanco para el mobiliario encastado. Placas sintéticas de cuarzo en color blanco y vidrio laminado trasparente en los bañnos y hormigón visto en los pilares de la estructura vertical preexistente.

← Kitchen. Cocina.

←← View to kitchen with exposed concrete pillar. Vista a cocina con pilar de concreto expuesto.
← Bathroom with view to garden. Baño con vista al jardín.
↙ Open floor plan in bedroom and bathroom. Habitación y baño con planta abierta.
↓ Bedroom. Habitación.

Typical of Spanish interior design is...

the relationship between
interior and exterior.

Casa in Sant Martí d'Empúrie

Habitan Arquitectos

Address: Carrer Baladre 16, Sant Martí d'Empúries, 17130 L'escala, Girona. **Client:** Nicola Chidichino. **Completion:** 2006. **Main function:** Home. **Materials:** Galvanized painted expanded metal, painted polyurethane and galician slate floor, metallic carpentries, gresite gray baths.

Three "boxes" placed on an exterior platform open or close up to relate to the exterior and to the indoor swimming pool. During the day time the façade surfaces hide in the housing boxes and disappear, this way the interior space and the exterior get confused, it is at the time when the porch created by the projecting one in the south is extended to the whole zone by day. The children's area was designed as a flexible space, with a dressing room and a bathroom, which can be opened or closed whenever desired, thus creating two separate rooms. The metallic sheet deployé housing modules have been painted in dark gray oxirón to contrast with the white walls and therefore to emphasize its function and at the same time create a façade.

Tres cajas colocadas sobre la plataforma se abren o se cierran para relacionar el espacio exterior y la piscina con el interior. De día los cerramientos se esconden en las cajas y desaparecen, así el espacio interior y el exterior se confunden, es entonces cuando el porche creado por el voladizo en el sur se amplía a toda la zona de día. La zona de noche es en cambio un espacio compacto e introvertido. La zona de los niños ha sido concebida como un único espacio que se separa en dos mediante un vestidor y un baño que puede cerrarse o abrirse según convenga. Los módulos de chapa metálica deployé se han pintado de gris oscuro oxirón para contrastar con el blanco de los muros y por tanto destacar su diferencia de función y a la vez componer las fachadas.

← Entrance view. Vista desde la entrada.

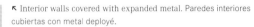
↖ Interior walls covered with expanded metal. Paredes interiores cubiertas con metal deployé.
↑ Dining room. Comedor.
← Interior view. Vista interna.
↓ First floor plan. Primera planta.
↗ Living room with open views to garden. Salón con vista hacia al jardín.
↘ Front façade. Fachada principal.
↘↘ Detail of interior courtyard. Detalle del patio interior.

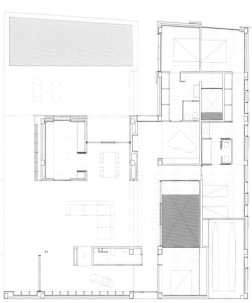

Typical of Spanish interior design is...

the combination of luxury,
functionality and technology.

Concrete House II

A-cero

Location: Pozuelo de Alorcón, Madrid. **Completion:** 2010. **Main function:** Home. **Materials:** Concrete, wood and glass.

This big single-family house in the outskirts of Madrid on a 5,000 square meter plot has a 1,600 square meters built surface on a one-storey building. The house appears to be hidden between concrete walls and vegetable ramps that extend up to the roof. They are dyed in dark gray and contain, between them, vegetation areas that seem to climb towards the sky. The back front of the house is totally opened towards the garden where the lounge, dining room, library, study and bedrooms are. In this façade the wide windows, the volumes set and the projections (made of concrete) too enhance. The large window of the main lounge hides itself automatically in order to make this stay completely opened to the exterior areas.

Esta casa unifamiliar en las afueras de Madrid sobre una superficie de 5,000 metros cuadrados tiene 1,600 metros cuadrados construidos sobre un piso. La primera sensación que produce esta casa al entrar en su terreno es que pareciera que está oculta entre muros de concreto y rampas de vegetación que se extienden hacia el techo. Están pintados de negro y contienen, entre ellos, áreas de vegetación que parecen escalar hacia el cielo. La fachada de la casa muestra una visión orgánica espectacular de la casa en conjunto. La parte de atrás de la casa, en donde se encuentran la sala de estar, el comedor, la biblioteca, el estudio y los dormitorios, estan totalmente abiertos al jardín. El terreno también incluye un jardín elegante y un pequeño lago.

← Working area with floating staircase. Zona de trabajo con escalera flotante.

↖ Kitchen featuring slightly eccentric angles and a center island stove.
La cocina que destaca ángulos ligeramente excéntricos y una isla en el centro.
↑ Interior passage. Corredor interior.
← Kitchen. Cocina.
↓ First floor plan. Primera planta.
↗ Living room. Salón.
↘ Kitchen with island stove. Cocina isla.
↘↘ Exterior view. Vista hacia el exterior.

Typical of Spanish interior design is...

unavoidably exuberant and
un-abashedly outrageous.

Casa Son Vida

Marcel Wanders, Moooi / tecARCHITECTURE

Location: Mallorca. **Luxury residential developer:** Cosmopolitan Estates. **Completion:** 2010. **Main function:** Home. **Furniture:** B&B Italia, Cappellini, Baccarat, Poliform, and Moooi.

Casa Son Vida is in fact a reno of a 1960s Mediterranean villa, but it has been turned into an fantastic, sprawling luxury residence, designed to attract the young, discerning and bold, who are confident and design-savvy enough to know what they are looking at. The handiwork of Marcel Wanders is evident everywhere in the Casa that looks a bit like an unruly movie set with its dino-bone exterior staircase, and various bits and pieces that remind you of Tomorrowland, Mickey Mouse, Finding Nemo and, of course, Alice in Wonderland. With its retro synthetic vibe, the house clashes happily with its lush surroundings, but the interior, in its white-dominant serenity is much less startling, although fun and unexpected detail is found in every space. There is absolutely nothing ordinary in this house. Everything is customized, every aspect considered a million times. It is a great example or considered chaos.

Casa Son Vida es un chalet del Mediterráneo de los años 60 que ofrece un exterior carismático que transgrede las limitaciones del sitio y del contexto, redefiniendo el concepto de lujo. La obra manual de Marcel Wanders es evidente por todas partes en el Casa que parece un poco un juego de película rebelde con su hueso de dinosaurio la escalera exterior, y varios añicos y pedazos que le recuerdan de Tomorrowland, Mickey Mouse, Encuentro Nemo y, desde luego, Alicia en el País de las Maravillas. Con su vibración retro sintética, los choques de casa felizmente con su entorno lozano, pero el interior, en su serenidad blanca dominante son mucho menos alarmantes, aunque la diversión y el detalle inesperado sean encontrados en cada espacio. No hay absolutamente nada ordinario en esta casa.

← Living room. Sala de estar.

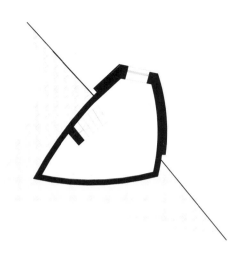

↖ Master bathroom. Baño principal.
↑ Floor plan. Planta.
← Living spaces placed underneath the arc. Salón ubicado debajo del arco.
↗ Master suite set right at the top of the structure. Master suite ubicado en lo alto de la estructura.
↘ Bird's eye view. Vista panorámica.
↘↘ Master bathroom, view to shower. Baño principal con vista a la ducha.

Typical of Spanish interior design is...
the contrast between the
contemporary and the classical.

Casa Mataró

Elia Felices Interiorismo

Address: Camí de Santa Rita 19, 08304 Mataró. **Completion:** 2008. **Main function:** Home. **Materials:** Ceramic, wood and mirror in furniture, stone in kitchen, stainless steel and lacquer furniture.

Behind an old monumental façade, a cozy home was created, and simultaneously an art gallery, located in the suburbs of Mataró (Barcelona). In the ground floor is the lobby. A couple of restored rocking chairs, a draped sofa in blue color baroque índigo and a coffee table with a polished mirror surface. Sober walls in gray, "le nouveau noir". In the lounge – dining room the glass coffee table, lightly oval and central foot of stainless finished polished steel mirror creates a contrast with the baroque molding chairs and with the floral and satiny motives. The curtains in black and white grant scenic character to the room. In the top lounge two mirror-like buckets as small tables, two armchairs restored in baroque moldings and a sofa with organic moldings with black velvet cushions, gramophones of the period, a lamp on a console in the style of Louis XIV, painted in black and a monumental portrait which is reflected before the baroque golden molding mirror. The mixture of periods and styles provide personality to the house.

Detrás una vieja fachada monumental, se crea un hogar acogedor, y a la vez galería de arte, situada a las afueras de Mataró (Barcelona). En la planta baja encontramos el recibidor. Un par de balancines restaurados, un sofá tapizado color azul índigo barroco y una mesa de centro con acabado en pulido espejo. Paredes sobrias en gris, "le nouveau noir". En el salón-comedor la mesa de centro, con sobre de vidrio, ligeramente ovalado y pie central de acero inoxidable acabado pulido espejo crea un contraste con las sillas de molduras barrocas, motivos florales y satinados. Las cortinas en blanco y negro otorgan carácter escénico a la sala. En el salón superior dos cubos espejados como mesitas, dos sillones restaurados de molduras barrocas y un sofá con molduras orgánicas con cojines de terciopelo negro, gramófonos de época, lámpara de sobremesa sobre una consola estilo Louis XIV lacada en negro y un monumental retrato que se refleja ante el gran espejo de moldura barroca dorada. La mezcla de épocas y estilos dotan de personalidad a la casa.

← Living room. Sala de estar.

↖ View to dining table from kitchen. Vista al comedor desde la cocina.
↑ Dining room. Comedor.
← Interior walls in gray, "le nouveau noir". Paredes sobrias en gris, "le nouveau noir".
↗ Interior with a Louis XIV style table and a monumental painting. Interior con consola al estilo Louis XIV lacada en negro y una pintura monumental.
↘ Living room with restored barroque airmchairs and a golden molding mirror. Salón con sillones restaurados de molduras barrocas y espejo de moldura dorada.
↘↘ Exterior view. Vista hacia el exterior.

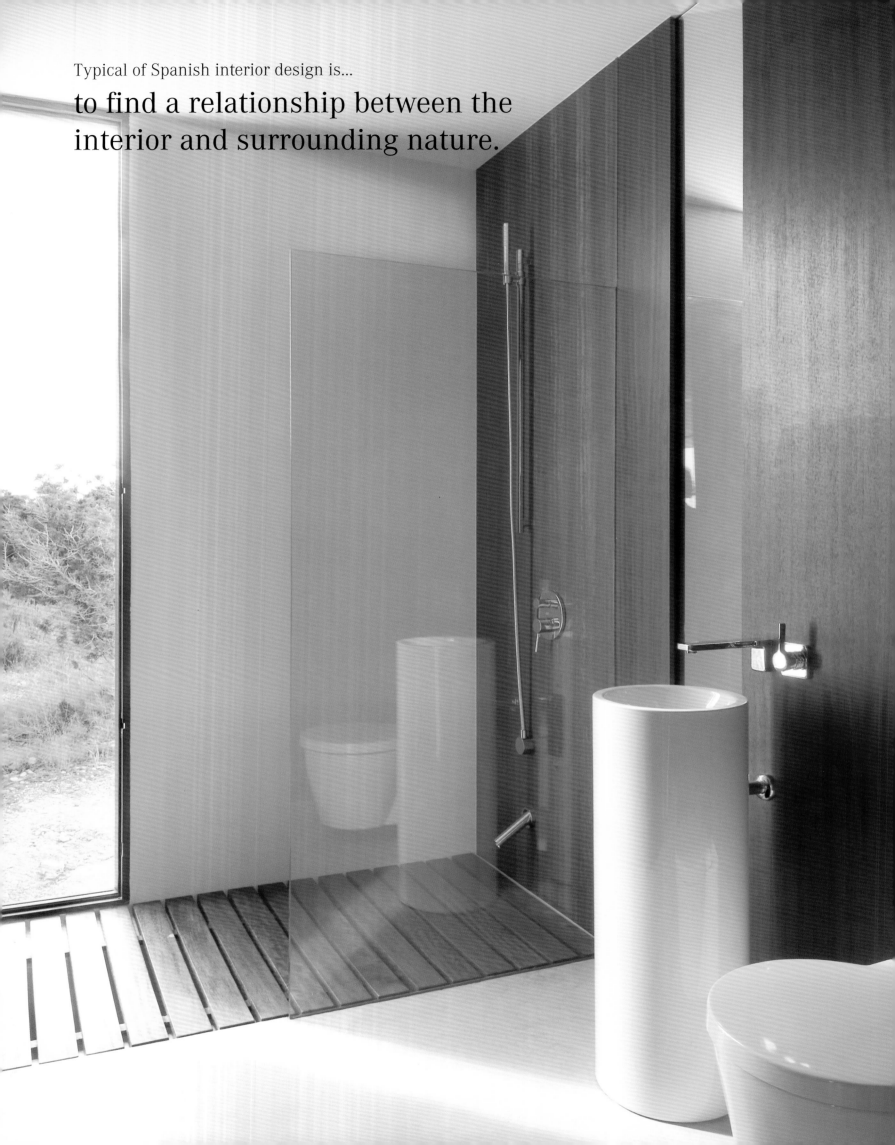

Typical of Spanish interior design is...

to find a relationship between the interior and surrounding nature.

Home Office in Formentera Island

Marià Castelló Martínez, arquitecte

Address: Camí Vell de la Mola km. 2, 3 Formentera. **Completion:** 2008. **Main function:** Living/working. **Materials:** Glass and iroko timber wood.

The building, a strictly geometrical structure of 12 x 12 meters, nestles between the existing vegetation and a remnant of a traditionally crafted drystone wall. This architecture seeks contextualization by way of interaction with the surroundings, echoing the traditional Formentera architecture, yet avoiding mimicry. The north-south orientation of the design creates the duality present in the program: the separation of public activity from private life. The architectural studio is located in the northernmost part, which is also the most exposed side. Natural northern light floods the space throughout the day. The priority with this space was to avoid any sense of confinement. The architect did this by opening up one of the walls to draw the natural surroundings inside.

El inmueble, una estructura estrictamente geométrica de 12 x 12 metros, se acomoda entre la vegetación existente y un muro de piedra original. La intervención busca refugio entre la vegetación existente y un fragmento de muro de piedra colocada en seco. Son estas dos directrices las que condicionan las dimensiones, la orientación y la altura total de una edificación de geometría austera que guarda paralelismos con la tradición arquitectónica de Formentera. Un muro de piedra seca de factura tradicional establece las directrices de alineación en el territorio y se convierte en parte del alzado norte del edificio, travándolo en el paisaje. Una vieja capilla de cisterna determina. El eje longitudinal de la intervención, siendo un referente objeto de diálogo tensión constante desde el exterior como desde el interior. Una arquitectura que busca la contextualidad a través de las relaciones con el entorno, apartándose del mimetismo.

← Bathroom with view to surroundings. Baño con vista al entorno.

↖ Office. Oficina.
↑ Hallway. Pasillo.
← Bedroom. Habitación.
↗ Guest room. Habitación de invitados.
↘ Front façade. Fachada principal.
↘↘ Detail of kitchen in guest room. Detalle de la cocina en habitación de invitados.

Typical of Spanish interior design is...
to connect the interior with the exterior surroundings.

House at the Pyrenees

Cadaval & Sola-Morales

Location: Canejan, Valle de Aran. **Completion:** 2010. **Main function:** Home. **Materials:** Wood and glass.

Located in a small town in the Pyrenees, Canejan, Catalonia, this dry stone house is a comfortable residence that consists of two units within one envelope. It features impressive views over the valley, whereas an identical window at the ceiling, allows views to the summit mountain. The design of the house not only respects the envelope, but also the historical values of the architecture. The new technologies and knowledge of age are applied to create a sustainable house, even in an extreme climate.

Ubicada en un pequeño pueblo anidado en los Pirineos, Canejan, Cataluña, esta casa de piedra seca es una cómoda residencia que tiene dos unidades en un solo sobre. Cuenta con impresionantes vistas sobre el valle, mientras que una ventana idéntica en la parte superior del techo, permite ver la cumbre de la montaña. El diseño de la casa no sólo respeta el sobre, sino también los valores históricos de la arquitectura. Las nuevas tecnologías y conocimientos de edad se aplican para hacer la casa sostenible, incluso en un clima extremo.

← Living room with fireplace. Sala de estar con chimenea.

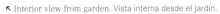

↖ Interior view from garden. Vista interna desde el jardín.
↑ Dining room. Comedor.
← Kitchen with views to surroundings. Cocina con vista hacia el entorno.
↗ Second living room with "Fire-Orb" and terrace. Segunda sala de estar con chimenea "Fire-Orb" y terraza.
↘ Interior view. Vista interna.
↘↘ Floor plans. Plantas.

Typical of Spanish interior design is...
to keep the scale and presence
of the existing.

House in a Former Barn in the Alt Empordà

Habitan Arquitectos

Address: Carrer Closes 3, 17474 Vilamacolum. **Client:** Gonzalo Vilaseca & Janine Kraue. **Completion:** 2007, original: 1920. **Main function:** Home. **Materials:** "Tova" on ceramics floors and industrial parquet, exposed concrete ceiling, balconies of sheet of scaffolding.

This unifamiliar house chooses to maintain its envelope, the perimetral walls and the original openings, in which two rectangular concrete volumes were built to house the program. In the ground floor, a curved wall approaches or separates from the perimeter depending on the light shapes the stays. On the other hand in the first floor plan the wall is closed on if same forming the different rooms that connect with the exterior across interior balconies done with plates of scaffolding. These terraces extend in the exterior and there they transform in a balcony traversed to south with a view to the most distant landscape. The baths have a glass front that allows to take as a sight of bottom the wall of stone and the vertical garden accompanying to the tub. The finished ones are neutral, little elaborated to leave the protagonism to the spaces, especially the intermediate ones. Under the cover there is opened a great diaphanous space that is the office.

Este proyecto de vivienda opta por mantener el envoltorio, es decir el muro perimetral y las aberturas originales saneándolos y se construyen en el interior dos forjados rectan This unifamiliar house chooses to maintain its envelope, the perimetral walls and the original openings, in which two rectangular concrete volumes were built to house the program. In the ground floor, a curved wall approaches or separates from the perimeter depending on the light shapes the stays. On the other hand in the first floor plan the wall is closed on if same forming the different rooms that connect with the exterior across interior balconies done with plates of scaffolding. These terraces extend in the exterior and there they transform in a balcony traversed to south with a view to the most distant landscape. The baths have a glass front that allows to take as a sight of bottom the wall of stone and the vertical garden accompanying to the tub. The finished ones are neutral, little elaborated to leave the protagonism to the spaces, especially the intermediate ones. Under the cover there is opened a great diaphanous space that is the office.

← Balconies seen from the living room. Los balcones vistos desde la sala de estar.

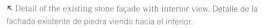

↖ Detail of the existing stone façade with interior view. Detalle de la fachada existente de piedra viendo hacia el interior.

↑ Intermediate spaces and bathtub window facing the stone wall. Espacios intersticiales y ventana de la bañera dando al muro de piedra.

← Kitchen. Cocina.

↗ Attic. Buhardilla.

↘ First floor plan. Planta baja.

↘↘ View of the original wall between two walls. Vista del muro original entre dos muros.

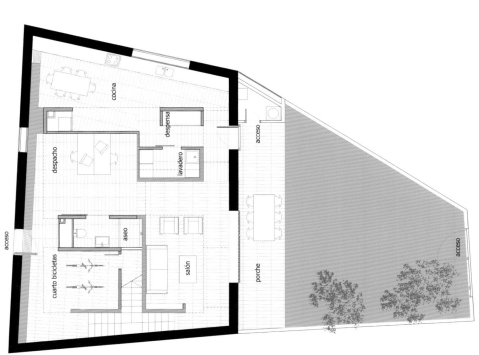

Typical of Spanish interior design is...

a diaphanous and functional
distribution.

Vivienda 4

A-cero

Location: Pozuelo de Alarcón, Madrid. **Completion:** 2009. **Main function:** Home. **Materials:** Silk wallpaper, exotic woods.

Continuing with the elegant style and organized of A-cero, the interior of the construction stands out for a diaphanous and functional distribution that is divided into two taking the main entry as a reference point. In the left wing are the most private stays (four bedrooms (with their own bathrooms) a playroom and a small living room) and on the right side are the most public areas; the living room with a considerable height which communicates with the dining room in two different environments. Both open up to the garden, porch and swimming pool across large windows, which close to an interior courtyard contribute to the great interior lighting.

Continuando con el estilo elegante y ordenado de A-cero, el interior de la construcción se destaca por una distribución diáfana y funcional que se divide en dos tomando como referencia la entrada principal. En el ala izquierda se localizan las estancias más privadas (cuatro dormitorios (con sus respectivos baños) un cuarto de juegos y una salita de estar) y en la derecha se encuentran las estancias más públicas. En esta área se destacan especialmente los espacios amplios y abiertos, como el salón con una altura considerable que se comunica con el comedor en dos ambientes diferenciados. Ambos se abren al jardín, porche y piscina a través de grandes ventanales, que junto a un patio interior aportan una gran luminosidad a la vivienda.

← Living room with open façade towards garden. Sala de estar con fachada abierta hacia el jardín.

←← View to sculpture in main living room. Vista a la escultura en la sala de estar principal.
← Entrance area. Vestíbulo.
↑ Floor plan. Planta.
↙ Dining room. Comedor.
↓ Lounge/porch. Salón/pórtico.

shopping

Typical of Spanish interior design is...

to show off the virtues of a constructional system through a material.

Heaven Showroom

Capella Garcia Arquitectura

Address: Port Forum, Barcelona. **Client:** Resyrok. **Completion:** 2008. **Main function:** Showroom. **Materials:** Vinyl membrane, color modification through electronically-programmed LEDs [RGB].

"Heaven" is the title of an ephemeral space whose purpose is to show off the virtues of a constructional system using vinyl, developed by the Resyrok Company. It invites the visitor to travel along a tunnel revealing the material's varied possibilities. There are two openings in the façade: one of them, which comes forward to receive the visitor, is the entrance, and the other, which seems to retreat from the visitor, is the exit. The interior lighting keeps changing color and shade, making the plastic membrane into something living. As one enters, one goes through a large dome where an oscillating lamp hangs like a tonsil. In one place, the glossy-finish plastic material looks like a painted wall and reflects the light; in another, the same material, but this time with a translucent finish and illuminated from behind, turns the walls into a great lamp that keeps taking on different colors, through a system of electronically-programmed LEDs [RGB].

"Heaven" es el título de un espacio efímero cuyo objetivo es de lucir las virtudes de un sistema de construcción usando vinyl, desarrollado por la empresa Resyrok. Este espacio invita al visitante a viajar a lo largo de un túnel que revela las posibilidades variadas del material. Hay dos aperturas en la fachada: una de ellas, se aproxima a recibir al visitante, sirve como entrada, y la otra, que parece retirarse del visitante, es la salida. La iluminación de interior sigue cambiando el color y la sombra, dandole vida a la membrana plástica. Al entrar y atravesar la cúpula, una lámpara oscilante cuelga como una amígdala. En ciertos puntos, el material de plástico de fin brillante parece como una pared pintada y refleja la luz; en oto punto, el mismo material, pero esta vez con un fin translúcido e iluminado por detras, convierte las paredes en una gran lámpara que sigue cambiando los colores con el uso de un sistema programado electrónicamente LEDs [RGB].

← Façade openings, as entrance and exit. Aperturas en la fachada como punto de entrada y salida.

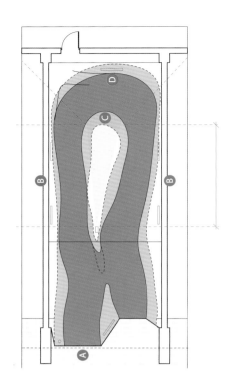

↖ Tunnel revealing the material's varied possibilities. Túnel que revela las posibilidades variadas del material.
↑ Floor plan. Planta.
← Translucent vinyl finish with pink backlit. Terminado de vinilo translúcido con iluminación detrás en color rosado.
↗ View from entrance to tunnels. Vista de la entrada hacia los túneles.
↘ Hyper-realistic effect at the end of tunnel. Efecto hiperrealista al final de túnel.
↘↘ View towards entrance/exit from interior. Vista hacia el punto de entrada/salida desde el interior.

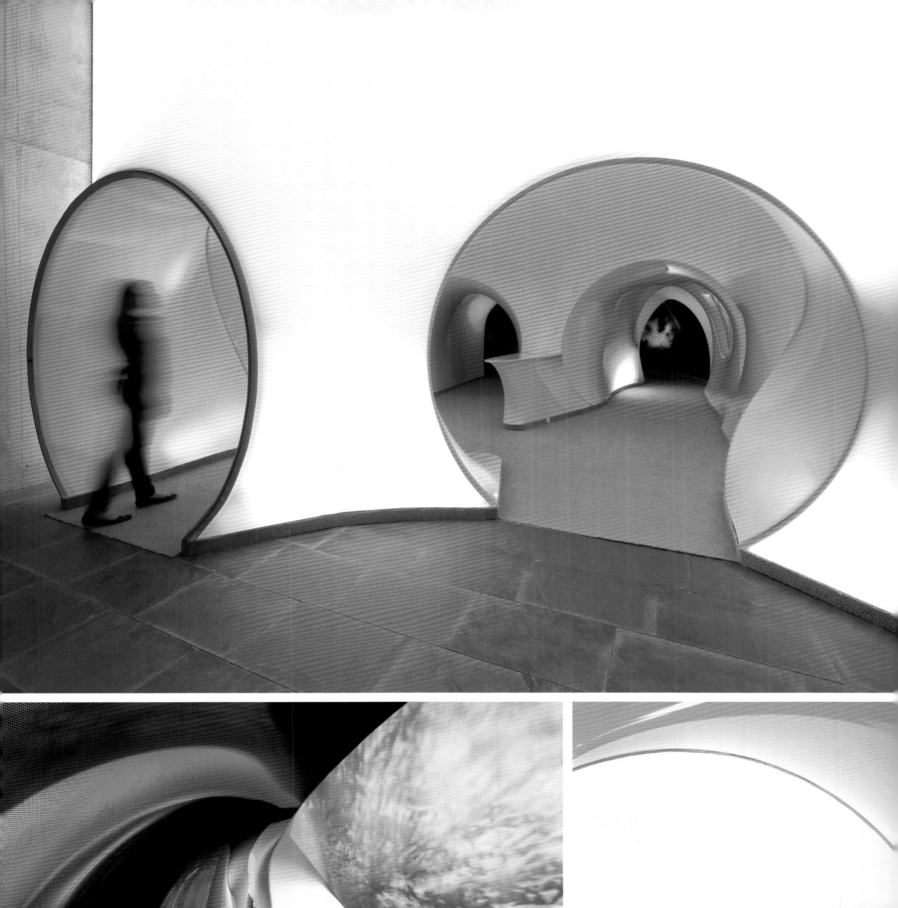
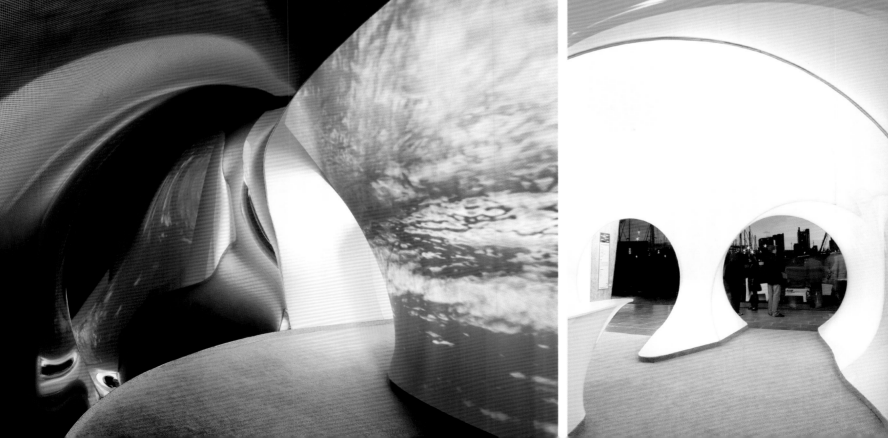

Typical of Spanish interior design is...

to think about the details without
conforming to the established codes.

Lurdes Bergada Flagship Store

Dear Design

Address: Centro Comercial L'Illa Diagonal, Avenida Diagonal 557, 08029 Barcelona. **Client:** Lurdes Bergada. **Completion:** 2009. **Main function:** Shop. **Materials:** Thin smoothed cement floor, birch plywood cement and natural varnished iron.

In keeping with the fashion brand's industrial and minimalistic style, Dear Design created a vast hangar-like feel by including all of the functions of the store – both client facing and back-room – under one roof, but separating them with a curving wall. This wall, created with 1,000 pieces of beech wood screwed together by 2,400 screws, forms an igloo-like huge presence and becomes a focal point that emphasizes the size of the entire space. Each piece of wood is unique and each piece is visibly numbered – a necessary technical detail for building the wall and a creative design idea to expose the "making of" and to bring attention to the construction features. The use of concrete, wood and cement further adds to the warehouse-like atmosphere.

De acuerdo con el estilo industrial minimalista de la marca de moda, Dear Design diseñó una estructura parecida a un perchero enorme, en donde aloja todas las funciones de la tienda – tanto los probadores y trastienda – bajo un mismo tejado, pero creando una separación con una pared curbeada. Este espacio lleno de luz presenta pues un gran contraste entre una estructura de madera que imita a una cueva de roca contemporánea y las paredes con aire industrial, las columnas de hormigón, los suelos de resina de acabado tosco, el techo visto y los bancos de madera inacabados. Const ruida con 1.000 piezas triangulares atornilladas entre sí con 2,400 tornillos, la piel de madera revela sus secretos constructivos que quedan vistos por su cara interior. Cada pieza triangular es única y está numerada para hacer la construcción más sencilla.

← Industrial-like hanging rack. Perchero al estilo industrial.

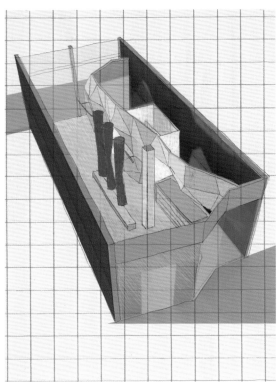

↖ Exposed construction details. Detalles de construcción expuestos.
↑ Bird's eye view of 3D model. Vista panorámica del modelo tridimensional.
← Detail of beech wood wall. Detalle de pared de madera de haya.
↗ View to wall created with 1,000 pieces of beech wood screwed together by 2,400 screws. Vista hacia la pared creada con 1,000 pedazos de madera de haya atornillada con 2,400 tornillos.
↘ Interior view. Vista interna.
↘↘ View to exposed screws in igloo-like structure. Vista hacia los tornillos expuestos en la estructura parecida a un iglú.

Typical of Spanish interior design is...

the coexistence between new
and old elements.

H&M

Estudio Mariscal

Address: Avigunda del Portal de l'Angel 22, 08002 Barcelona. **Completion:** 2008. **Interior and graphic design:** Estudio Mariscal. **Technical architecture and services:** MC Arquitectura e Ingeniería. **Lighting design:** iGuzzini. **Sculpture:** Taller de escultura Pere Casanovas. **Main function:** Shop. **Materials:** Metal, stone, marble and glass. **Furniture and textiles:** J. Mariscal for Uno Design (Guitar chair), stone-wool from Nani Marquina (Carpet), Constanza de Luceplan (lamp).

A 19th century building, listed as a vestige of the bourgeois architecture, and is the work of Domènech Estapà, now houses an H&M shop. The architects made the effort to reform the building, highlight the aspects which, over time and the different uses of the building in its latest stage, had been removed or altered. The dome, the three public rooms, the staircase well and the imperial staircase were kept. The interior design is composed of features that can be added and removed. A second exempt skin was superimposed on the old architecture, creating a new image, without blurring the original. This, which could have been an obstacle throughout the project, became an incentive as it finally helped the designers to achieve a multipurpose space which is flexible, modular and versatile.

Un edificio del siglo XIX, catalogado como un vestigio de la arquitectura burguesa, obra de Domènech Estapà, ahora aloja una tienda de H&M. Los arquitectos hicieron el esfuerzo para reformar el edificio, destacar los aspectos que con el tiempo y los diferentes empleos del edificio en su última etapa, habían sido alterados. La cúpula, los tres espacios públicos, la escalera con claraboya y la escalera imperial fueron conservadas. El diseño interior esta compuesto de elementos que pueden ser añadidos y extraidos. Una piel secundaria fue exenta y sobrepuesta sobre la arquitectura existente, creando una nueva imagen, sin enturbiar el original. Esto, que podría haber sido un obstáculo en todas partes del proyecto, se hizo un incentivo como esto finalmente ayudo a los diseñadores a alcanzar un espacio de fines múltiples que es flexible, modular y versátil.

← Main staircase. Escalera principal.

↖ Illuminated staircase at entrance. Escalera iluminada a la entrada.
↑ Paying counter. Mostrador de cajas.
← Underground floor. Piso subterráneo
↓ First and ground floor plan. Primera y planta baja.
→ View towards main staircase. Vista hacia escalera principal.
↘ Atrium. Atrio.
↘↘ Interior, women's section. Interior, sección para mujeres.

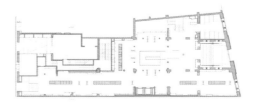

Typical of Spanish interior design is...

heritage is future.

Dat Bal Showroom

Estudio Antonio Jiménez Torrecillas

Address: Calle San Isidro, 18005 Granada. **Client:** Pilar Jiménez Torrecillas. **Completion:** 2006, original: 19th century. **Main function:** Showroom. **Materials:** Glass and Stainless steel.

To pop into Dal Bat Showroom is almost an obligation. Once inside, it gives the feeling of not having entered. This intervention hides the wooden panels that were originally concealed in old factories, exposes the ceilings that show structural demages, features pavements of former stables as a prolongation of the same street and features a hollow intact glass façade. The shop Dal Bat looks like a X-ray of the property. The floor surface, a sheet of aluminium serves as lighting support and glass trays seem to arise from the walls as exhibitors. The interior reveals the presence of new discreetly introduced elements that in its new relations with the existing do not border the survival of the idea. In Dal Bat the idea of adding consists in eliminating. Every conceptual addition is a subtraction, not an aggregation.

Asomarse a Dal Bat es como una obligación. Ya dentro, da la sensación de no haber entrado. Esta intervención suprime los revestimientos que ocultaban las irregulares fábricas originales, deja vistos los techos que denuncian sucesivas reparaciones estructurales urgentes, destaca los pavimentos de antiguas caballerizas como prolongación de la misma calle, trasdosa con vidrio dejando intactos los huecos a fachada. La tienda Dal Bat parece una radiografía del inmueble. Por lo demás, se ha dejado caer al suelo una chapa de aluminio como soporte de la luz y parecen surgir de las paredes bandejas de vidrio como expositores. El interior desvela la presencia de nuevos elementos discretamente introducidos que en sus novedosas relaciones con lo existente no limitan la pervivencia de la idea. En Dal Bat se añade eliminando. Cada adición conceptual es una sustracción, no una agregación.

← Detail of glass surface. Detalle de la superficie de cristal.

↖ Interior view. Vista interna.
↑ Product display. Demostración de producto.
← Window display. Escaparate.
↗ Interior view to gallery space. Vista interna de la galería.
↘ Sketch plan. Bosquejo de planta.
↘↘ Lighting installation. Instalación de iluminación.

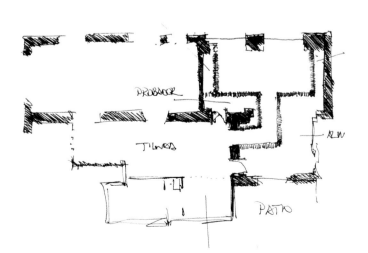

Typical of Spanish interior design is...
to think about the details without conforming to the established codes.

Munich Flagship Store

Dear Design

Address: Centro Comercial L'Illa Diagonal, Avenida Diagonal 557, 08029 Barcelona. **Client:** Berneda s.a. **Completion:** 2009. **Main function:** Shop. **Materials:** Dark glass surfaces, mirrors, metal trees and cage-like boxes hanging from the ceiling.

Established by the Berneda family in 1939, created its famous logo X in the 70s and it is currently recognized throughout the world as of the most creative brands of sports footwear. Dark-glass surfaces, mirrors, metal trees and cage-like boxes hanging from the ceiling (from which the shoes have "escaped"), all carry a carefree, experimental and impermanent air. The angular and clunky space with its hard edges and seemingly moving parts is clearly an attempt to say that the septuagenarian brand is nowhere near slowing down.

La marca Munich, fundada en 1939 por la familia Berneda, creó su famoso logo X en los años '70 y en la actualidad es reconocida mundialmente como una de las marcas más creativas de calzado deportivo. El espacio tiene un aire muy urbano gracias al color negro de paredes y suelos, y al diseño de formas angulares de los elementos expositivos. Multitud de espejos, mobiliario de fresno natural, árboles metálicos y cajas suspendidas, confieren al espacio un aire de renovación constante y movimiento.

← Angular, sloping shoe displays. Mostradores de zapatos angulares e inclinados.

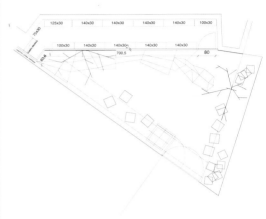

↖ Cage-like boxes as seating areas. Cajas parecidas a una jaula que funcionan como asientos.

↑ Floor plan. Planta.

← View to interior from shop window. Vista hacia el interior desde el escaparate.

↗ Dark glass surfaces, mirrors, metal trees and cage-like boxes hanging from the ceiling. Superficies oscuras de cristal, espejos, árboles metálicos y cajas parecidas a una jaula colgando del techo.

↘ Angular wooden counter. Mostrador angular de madera.

↘↘ Interior with shoes hanging from ceiling. Interior con zapatos colgados del techo.

Typical of Spanish interior design is...

defining boundaries between reality and illusion within one space.

Pharmacy in La Puebla 15

Buj+Colón Arquitectos

Address: Calle Pueblo 15, Palencia. **Completion:** 2010. **Main function:** Pharmacy. **Materials:** Myriad fibres and glass.

The Pharmacy in La Puebla 15 is decorated with large neon symbols illuminating both the interior and exterior. The designers have also removed the traditional pharmacy counter, placing medications alongside the customers. The project embraces the new demands for relationship and proximity of the customer with the product, breaking away from the classic formula of direct sales and creating an ambiance that places the medication on the same plane as the consumer. The interior and exterior zones are connected through a first filter that is interrupted to form shop windows, spaces for visual exchange where the façade increases in density and specificity.

La Farmacia en La Puebla 15 esta decorada con símbolos de neon luminosos grandes que iluminan tanto el interior como el exterior. Atendiendo a las nuevas exigencias de proximidad del cliente con el producto, el proyecto rompe con el esquema tradicional de venta y elimina el mostrador para situar los medicamentos en el lineal de venta, accesibles el consumidor. El interior, blanco y diáfano, con estanterías de cristal y acero, otorga todo el protagonismo a los productos en venta. El interior y zonas exteriores son unidos por un primer filtro que es interrumpido para formar escaparates, espacios para el cambio visual donde el façade aumenta en la densidad y la especificidad.

← Shelf display. Estantería.

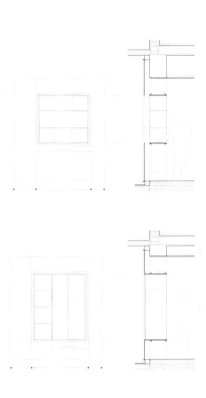

←← Exterior view by night. Vista exterior de noche.
← Interior illumination. Iluminación del interior.
↑ Wall detail. Detalle de la pared.
↙ Interior. Interior.
↓ Show window. Escaparate.

Typical of Spanish interior design is...

exploring the possibilities of a
material to create a magical space.

Joyeria D

Vaíllo & Irigaray + Galar

Address: Calle de Francisco Bergamín 7, 31003 Pamplona. **Lighting design:** ALS Lighting. **Client:** Danieli Joyeros. **Completion:** 2007. **Main function:** Shop. **Materials:** Metal plates (aluminum smelting) and wood.

A premise with scarce dimensions and deep and narrow geometry, is the frame of presentation of a collection of a jeweler's shop that is exposed in a dark space with magic airs, like a treasure chest. This container conforms by means of the macla of two opposite sections: superior, dark, dull, light and vibrant, and the lower silver, brilliant, heavy and rigid. The dark is generated by means of one asymmetric inverted U, which is generated like a vault, an extruded section, shaping thus the ceiling and the wings in an asymmetrical form, and proposing a reading like that of a mysteriously folded curtain. The other dihedral shapes the floor and the lateral furniture behind the counter, shaping a knocked down L. It is then generated as a folded spoiled, brilliant and deep surface.

Un local de escasas dimensiones y geometría profunda y estrecha, es el marco de presentación de una colección de joyería que se expone en un espacio oscuro con aires mágicos, a modo de cofre de los tesoros. Este contenedor se conforma mediante la macla de dos secciones contrapuestas: la superior, oscura, mate, ligera y vibrante, y la inferior plateada, brillante, pesada y rígida. La oscura se genera mediante una U asimétrica invertida, que genera a modo de bóveda, una sección extrudida, conformando de este modo el techo y los laterales, de forma asimétrica, y proponiendo una lectura a modo de cortinaje-telón misteriosamente plegado. El otro diedro conforma el suelo y el mobiliario lateral tras el mostrador central, conformando una L tumbada. Se genera como una superficie plegada desgastada, brillante y profunda.

← Interior with floating counter. Interior con mostrador flotante.

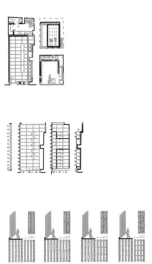

↖ Window slots. Ventanas con ranuras.
↑ Floor plans and wall details. Plantas y detalle de las paredes.
← Pleated DM wooden wall painted in black. Pared de madera DM plisada y lacadas en negro.
↗ Floating counter. Mostrador flotante.

Typical of Spanish interior design is...
to correlate simplicity and identity.

Munich Fractal Arena

Dear Design

Address: Calle Jorge Juan 10, 45006 Valencia. **Client:** Berneda s.a. **Completion:** 2010. **Main function:** Shop. **Materials:** A lacquered sheet of steel, tightened Barrisol ceiling for the lighting, white polyurethane floor with a glossy varnish and a white sheet of iron for the furniture.

Dear Design have completed this shop in Valencia with shoes displayed on a metal lattice for Spanish outfitters Munich. The wall-hung structure, which wraps around the perimeter of the shop, is inspired by the company's X-shaped logo and finished in lacquer. Munich Fractal Arena's interior is illuminated by a light diffuser spanning the ceiling, and entirely finished in glossy white resin floor, painted walls and lacquered furniture.

Dear Design ha completado esta tienda en Valencia con zapatos mostrados sobre un enrejado metálico para los abastecedores españoles de Munich. La estructura colgada por pared, que se envuelve alrededor del perímetro de la tienda, esta inspirada por el logo en forma de X de la empresa y terminada en la laca. El interior de Munich Fractal Arena eseta iluminado por un difusor ligero que atraviesa el techo, y completamente terminado en un piso blanco de resina brilloso, paredes pintadas y muebles laqueados.

← Display structure based on the repetition of the "X", symbol of the brand. Estructura de demostración basada en la repetición de la "X", símbolo de la marca.

↖ View to interior. Vista interna.
↑ Floor plan. Planta.
← Show window. Escaparate.
↗ Product floats in white, hollow structure and stands out in the space. Productos flotando en la estructura blanca con huecos y se destaca en el espacio.
↘ General view of structure display around interior. Vista general de la estructura que circunda el interior.

Index